D1613070

DUNDEE

A HISTORY AND CELEBRATION OF THE CITY

GILLIAN NICOLE FERGUSON

Produced by The Francis Frith Collection
exclusively for

OTTAKAR'S

www.ottakars.co.uk

First published in the United Kingdom in 2005
by The Francis Frith Collection®

Hardback Edition 2005
ISBN 1-84567-742-0

British Library Cataloguing in Publication Data

Dundee - A History and Celebration of the City
Gillian Nicole Ferguson

The Francis Frith Collection
Frith's Barn, Teffont,
Salisbury, Wiltshire SP3 5QP
Tel: +44 (0) 1722 716 376
Email: info@francisfrith.co.uk
www.francisfrith.co.uk

Printed and bound in England

Front Cover: **DUNDEE, THE ALEXANDRA FOUNTAIN 1907** D81001t

Additional modern photographs by Gillian Nicole Ferguson.

Domesday extract used in timeline by kind permission of
Alecto Historical Editions, www.domesdaybook.org
Aerial photographs reproduced under licence from
Simmons Aerofilms Limited.
Historical Ordnance Survey maps reproduced under licence from
Homecheck.co.uk

Every attempt has been made to contact copyright holders of illustrative material. We will be happy to give full acknowledgement in future editions for any items not credited. Any information should be directed to The Francis Frith Collection.

The colour-tinting in this book is for illustrative purposes only, and is not intended to be historically accurate

AS WITH ANY HISTORICAL DATABASE, THE FRANCIS FRITH ARCHIVE IS CONSTANTLY BEING CORRECTED AND IMPROVED, AND THE PUBLISHERS WOULD WELCOME INFORMATION ON OMISSIONS OR INACCURACIES

Contents

DUNDEE FROM THE AIR 1955 AFA61674BL

Historical Timeline for Dundee

c AD82
Roman camps at Perth and on the south banks of the Tay

Roman Britain

AD80 Agricola's invasion

208 Severus invades Caledonia

368 Theodosius defeats the Picts of Valentia

563 Columba lands at Iona

Dark Ages

761 Angus McFergus King of Dalriada and Strathclyde

841 Kenneth MacAlpine King of Scots

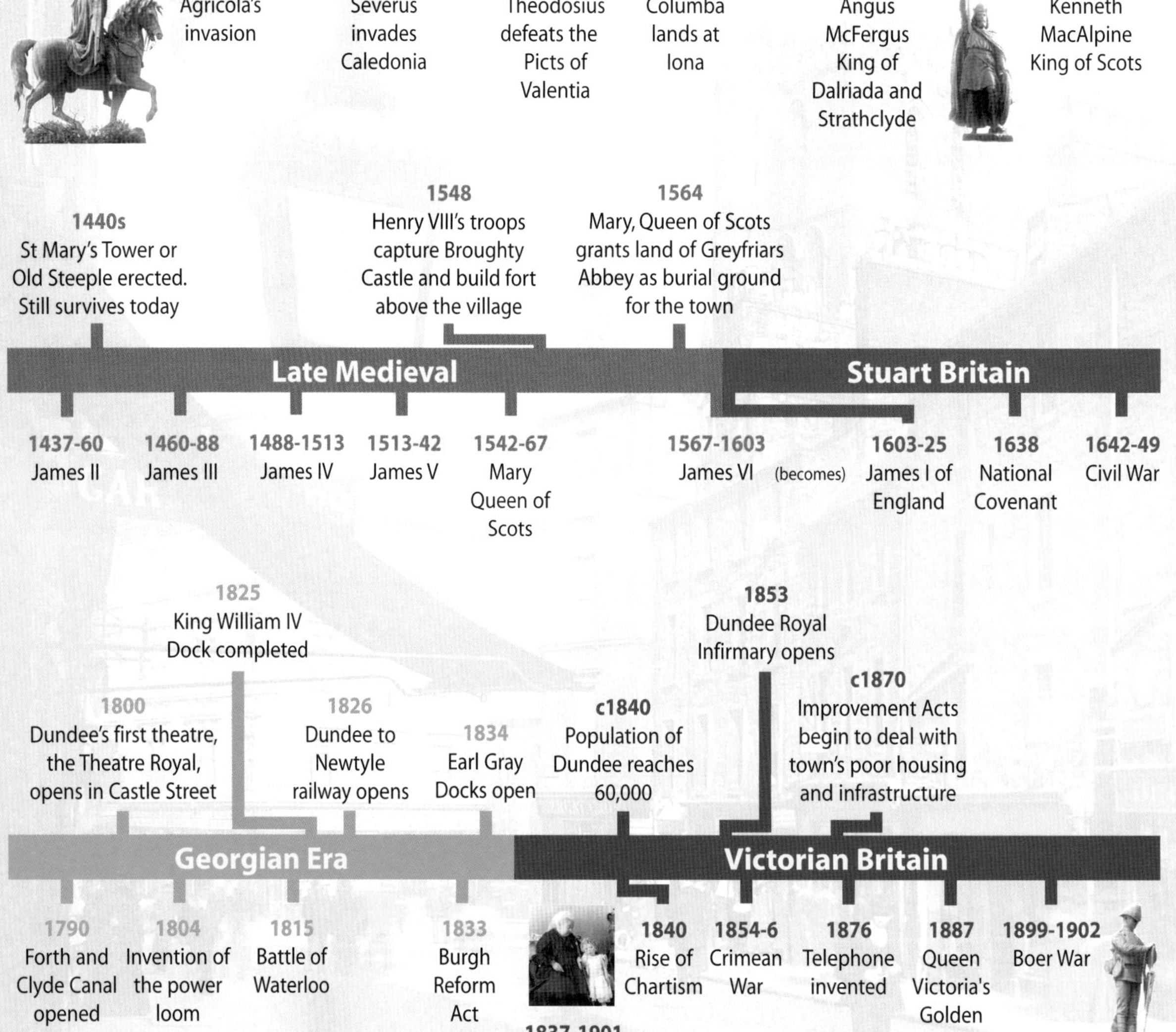

1440s
St Mary's Tower or Old Steeple erected. Still survives today

1548
Henry VIII's troops capture Broughty Castle and build fort above the village

1564
Mary, Queen of Scots grants land of Greyfriars Abbey as burial ground for the town

Late Medieval

1437-60 James II

1460-88 James III

1488-1513 James IV

1513-42 James V

1542-67 Mary Queen of Scots

1567-1603 James VI (becomes)

Stuart Britain

1603-25 James I of England

1638 National Covenant

1642-49 Civil War

1825
King William IV Dock completed

1800
Dundee's first theatre, the Theatre Royal, opens in Castle Street

1826
Dundee to Newtyle railway opens

1834
Earl Gray Docks open

c1840
Population of Dundee reaches 60,000

1853
Dundee Royal Infirmary opens

c1870
Improvement Acts begin to deal with town's poor housing and infrastructure

Georgian Era

1790 Forth and Clyde Canal opened

1804 Invention of the power loom

1815 Battle of Waterloo

1833 Burgh Reform Act

Victorian Britain

1837-1901 Queen Victoria

1840 Rise of Chartism

1854-6 Crimean War

1876 Telephone invented

1887 Queen Victoria's Golden Jubilee

1899-1902 Boer War

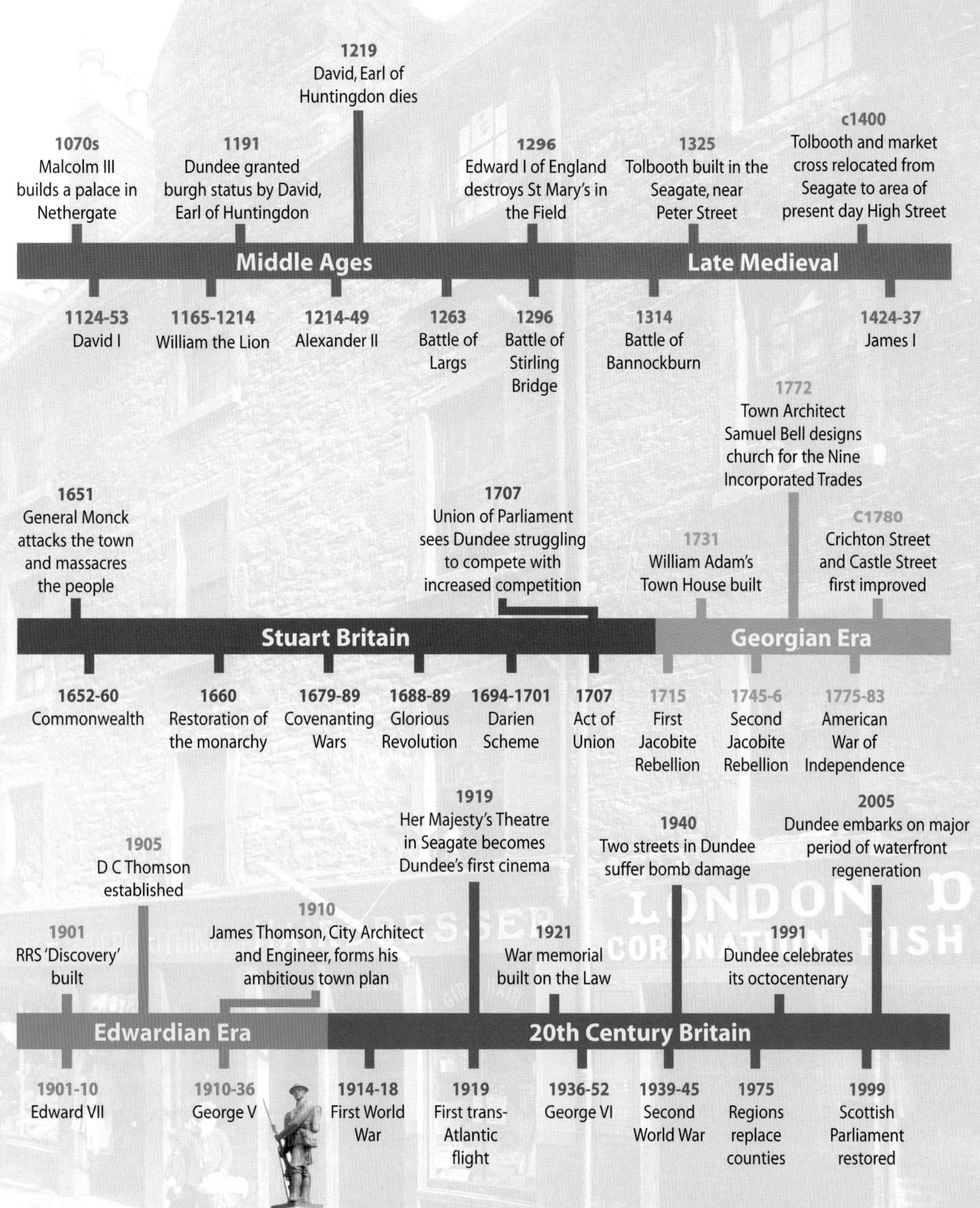
1070s
Malcolm III builds a palace in Nethergate
1191
Dundee granted burgh status by David, Earl of Huntingdon
1219
David, Earl of Huntingdon dies
1296
Edward I of England destroys St Mary's in the Field
1325
Tolbooth built in the Seagate, near Peter Street
c1400
Tolbooth and market cross relocated from Seagate to area of present day High Street
Middle Ages
Late Medieval
1124-53
David I
1165-1214
William the Lion
1214-49
Alexander II
1263
Battle of Largs
1296
Battle of Stirling Bridge
1314
Battle of Bannockburn
1424-37
James I
1651
General Monck attacks the town and massacres the people
1707
Union of Parliament sees Dundee struggling to compete with increased competition
1731
William Adam's Town House built
1772
Town Architect Samuel Bell designs church for the Nine Incorporated Trades
C1780
Crichton Street and Castle Street first improved
Stuart Britain
Georgian Era
1652-60
Commonwealth
1660
Restoration of the monarchy
1679-89
Covenanting Wars
1688-89
Glorious Revolution
1694-1701
Darien Scheme
1707
Act of Union
1715
First Jacobite Rebellion
1745-6
Second Jacobite Rebellion
1775-83
American War of Independence
1901
RRS 'Discovery' built
1905
D C Thomson established
1910
James Thomson, City Architect and Engineer, forms his ambitious town plan
1919
Her Majesty's Theatre in Seagate becomes Dundee's first cinema
1921
War memorial built on the Law
1940
Two streets in Dundee suffer bomb damage
1991
Dundee celebrates its octocentenary
2005
Dundee embarks on major period of waterfront regeneration
Edwardian Era
20th Century Britain
1901-10
Edward VII
1910-36
George V
1914-18
First World War
1919
First trans-Atlantic flight
1936-52
George VI
1939-45
Second World War
1975
Regions replace counties
1999
Scottish Parliament restored

A. LAWSON BUTCHER
WATSON

CHAPTER ONE

From Small Beginnings

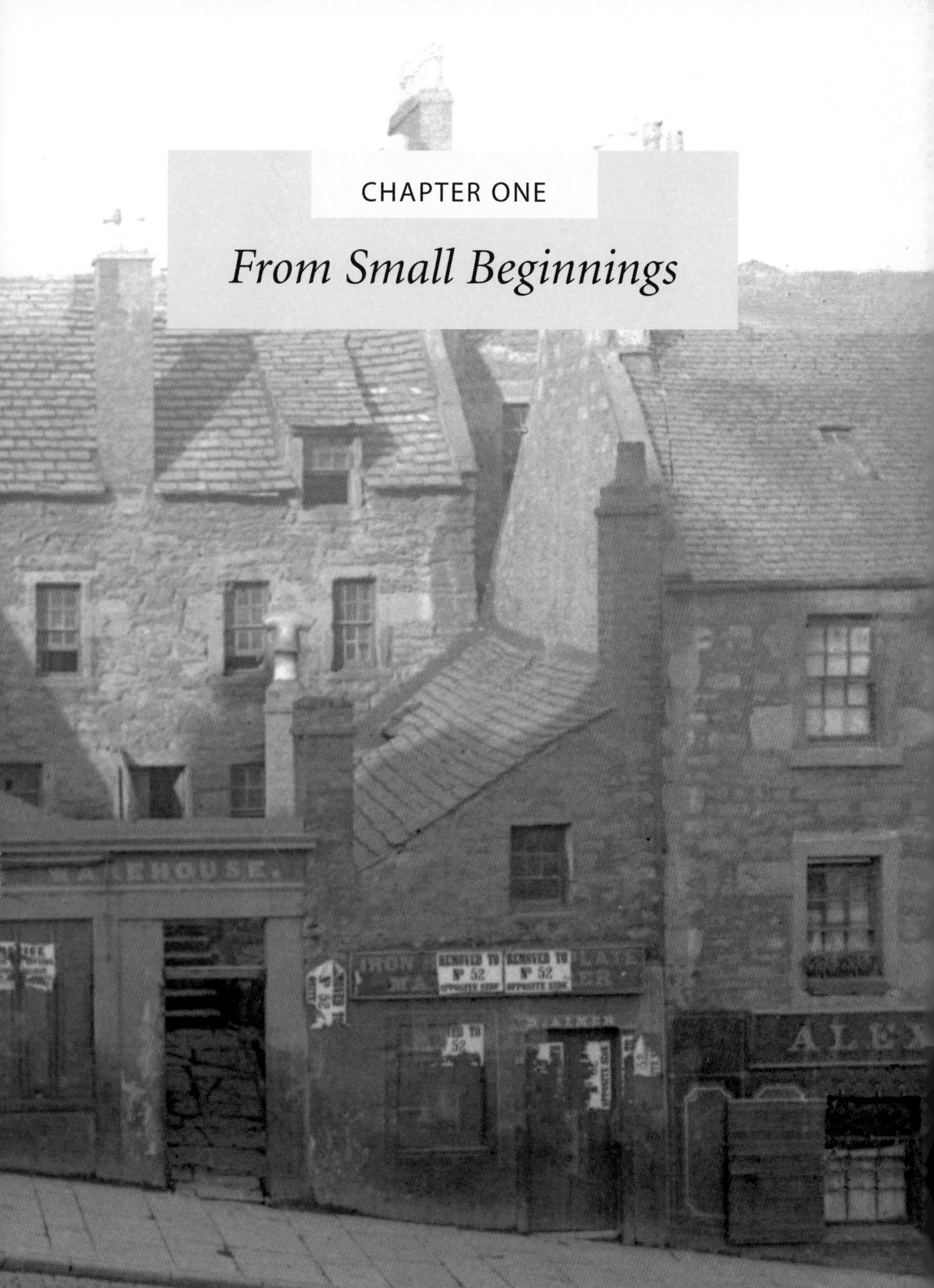

THE CITY OF DUNDEE, nestled beside the River Tay near the mouth of the river, has had a long and rich history. Although the name 'Dundee' can claim various origins, it is generally believed that it is related to the name of an Iron Age fort called Dun Diagh, which was located at the top of the Law. In ancient Gaelic, 'dun' meant hill or fort, and 'diagh' may have been the name of the local chief. Alternatively, the name may have its origins in the Celtic 'Duntaw,' which literally meant the 'hill on the Tay'. The Tay itself has played an integral role in the growth and fortunes of Dundee.

The Law, the hill that dominates the city's skyline, is all that remains of an ancient volcano formed approximately 400,000,000 years ago. The name 'Law' derives from the old Scot's word for hill. At nearly 600 feet above sea level, the Law is also one of the city's most prominent features, and commands a spectacular panorama of the city and the surrounding countryside. From its summit can be seen the Grampian mountain range in the north, the hills towards Perth in the west, the eastern suburb of Broughty Ferry, the Kingdom of Fife, and some of the best views of the 'Silvery Tay'.

The banks of the Tay would have been a natural place for people to settle. The first peoples to use the area were probably nomadic hunter-gatherers, fishing the fertile waters, gathering shellfish on the raised beaches, and hunting in the surrounding woodland. Evidence for the very earliest human activity, around 8,000 years ago, has been found in shell middens, flint scatters and traces of

DUNDEE AND THE RIVER TAY 1938 SA000127 (Courtesy of University of St Andrews Library)

primitive tool making. At Stannergate in 1878 evidence of a flint-knapping site was found, along with a midden full of shells, red deer antler, burnt wood and porpoise bones. Around the fourth millennium BC, an agricultural society began to form; the many stone axes found in the area suggest that the first farmers to settle on the banks of the Tay estuary would have had to clear the land of trees to create their fields.

The site of present-day Dundee would have been chosen as a settlement because it was naturally an easy place to defend. The summits of many of the hills around the city show remains of massive fortifications, which formed a protective arc around Dundee. The summit of the Law was crowned with one of these defensive forts, although little of it can now be seen. At the water's edge stood Black Rock, later Castle Rock, on the site of present day Castle Street, with cliffs on its seaward side. Black Rock occupied a central position in a wide bay with rocky outcrops to the west. It was on Black Rock that some of the earliest settlers constructed a fort. There were several fresh water streams in the area, essential to the growth of the settlement.

Dundee's Dragon

To the north of Dundee, near Balluderon, sits the Pictish Martin's Stone, carved with symbols including a serpent or dragon. Legend has it that a local farmer from Pitempton was lucky enough to be blessed with nine beautiful daughters. One day he sent the youngest out to fetch water from the local well. When she did not return he sent another daughter, and another, until all nine maidens were missing. Wondering if they were playing some kind of game with him, he set off to find them, only to make the horrifying discovery of a great dragon picking over the remains of every one of his daughters. Running for his life, he managed to tell his story to his neighbours. A bold lad, Martin, who had loved the farmer's eldest daughter, pledged to rid the countryside of the beast and avenge his lost love. Martin attacked the beast and killed it, and the spot where it fell is marked with Martin's Stone.

THE DRAGON SCULPTURE 2005
D81701k (Gillian Ferguson)

The Romans had campaigned in Scotland between the late 1st and 3rd centuries AD. The most successful campaigns were probably Agricola's of AD 82 and AD 86, when he built camps at Perth and on the south bank of the Tay. Also, signs of a marching camp have been found at Longforgan, to the west of Dundee, on the route taken by Septimius Severus in AD 208. However, although the Romans were never to gain a strong foothold within Scotland, their presence united the various tribes; one of the first kings of a united Scotland, Donald I, is reputed to have built a stronghold at Castle Rock. The merging of the Picts and the Scots into one nation during the 10th and 11th centurys saw further rulers, such as King Edgar and Malcolm III, bring their travelling courts to Dundee during their reigns.

The landscape of early Dundee is almost unrecognisable today owing to the reclamation of land and to the removal of some of the smaller hills and rocky outcrops which had previously prohibited the town's growth. For many years, the settlement around Castle Rock remained small, with the inhabitants eking a living

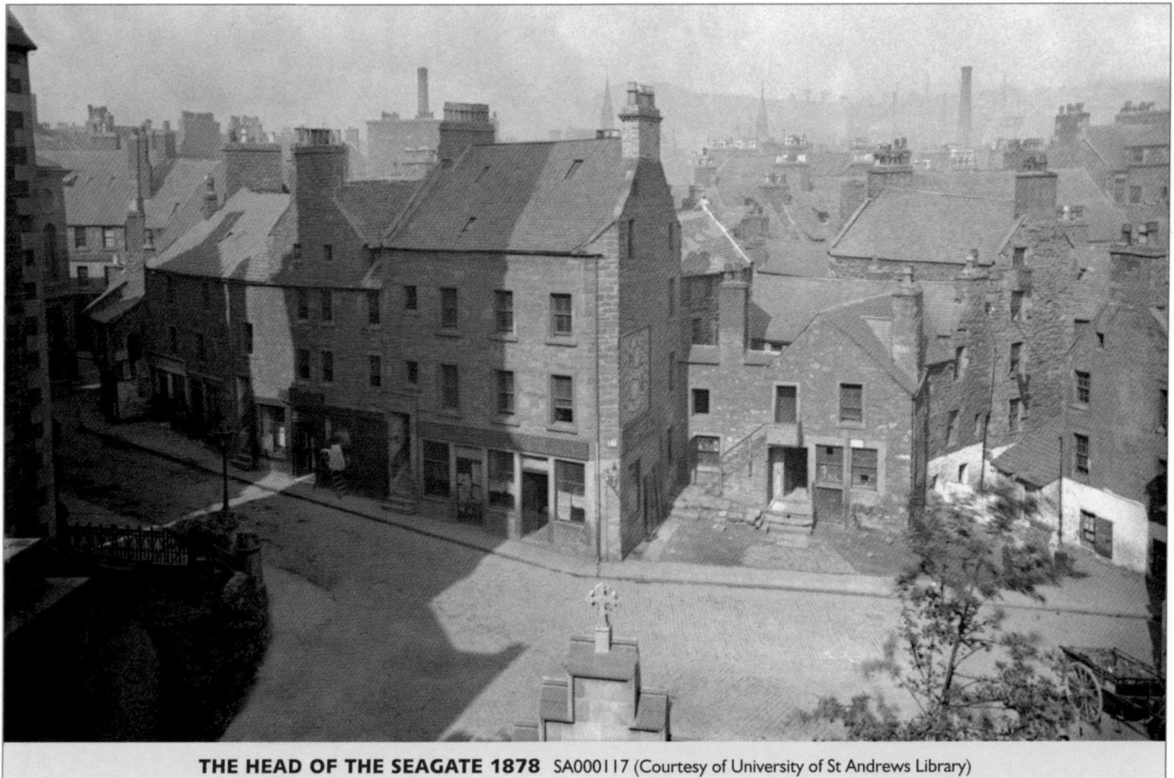

THE HEAD OF THE SEAGATE 1878 SA000117 (Courtesy of University of St Andrews Library)

Although the houses in this photograph are not medieval, the plots of land on which they stand, or 'rigs' as they are known in Scotland, had probably remained much the same since medieval times. The buildings pictured here were demolished in the late 19th century with the creation of Commercial Street.

from farming, fishing and hunting. Trade with other local communities existed only in the surplus from these activities, and few of Dundee's inhabitants would have travelled outwith the immediate area. The first street to be settled was probably the Seagate, where the Scouring Burn and Dens Burn ran. The buildings here would have been little more than wooden huts, probably built of wattle and daub, with roofs thatched with turf. The next street to develop was the Cowgate. The Lady Well, the town's most used water source, was at the bottom of the Hilltown. The Hilltown, or 'Rotten Row' as it was known, lay outside the town. The regular market at the foot of the Hilltown certainly annoyed the authorities, as goods were sold here without paying the town's taxes.

In 1070, King Malcolm III married Margaret, great-niece of Edward the Confessor of England. Malcolm built a royal palace to the west of the settlement for his bride in what is now the Nethergate. At the time, the palace sat on its own

THE FOOT OF BONNET HILL, NOW HILLTOWN c1878 SA000136 (Courtesy of University of St Andrews Library)

The Hilltown was originally known as Bonnet Hill, and lay outwith Dundee until the barony was purchased by the town in 1699. The left-hand building is a butcher's; note the window display with sides of meat. The handcart was probably used for deliveries - not an enviable job if your destination was the 'top o' the Hill'!

away from the hustle and bustle, but soon wooden buildings began to appear on the eastern side of Castle Rock in what was to become the High Street. It was Earl David of Huntingdon, William the Lion's brother, who elevated Dundee to the status of a burgh in 1191, although no charter survives. Dundee then began to expand rapidly because of growing trade with the Earl's wealthy estates in England. The town was the only trade port owned by the Earl, and was given exemption from tariffs at English ports; for this reason the port at Dundee was used by traders from all over the surrounding countryside. Also, Dundee harbour had the natural advantage of being sheltered compared to the harbour at Arbroath, and much deeper than the river at Perth.

By the time of Earl David's death in 1219, Dundee had become a busy and important port with many fine houses, a grammar school, and residents from as far afield as France, with ships visiting from Holland and Scandinavia. The Seagate was still the most important street within the town, and when Robert I granted a piece of land where a tolbooth could be built in 1325, it was probably situated where Peter Street meets the Seagate today. The market cross was also first situated in the Seagate; the site is still marked today with a cross pattern built into the cobbles at the bottom of Peter Street. The main exports from the town were sheepskins and wool, which were sent to the Netherlands – they were much in demand for the Flemish cloth industries. Farmers came to Dundee from the surrounding rural areas to sell their sheepskins and in turn buy items such as iron or salt that had to be brought from outwith the area.

Did you know?

Dundee's Shoreline: The Seagate Today

The shoreline in Dundee was originally much higher, running just in front of the Seagate and the bottom of Castle Street. Dundee's docks were built almost wholly on reclaimed land, and these docks were later filled in, so that today Dundee stretches much further into the Tay.

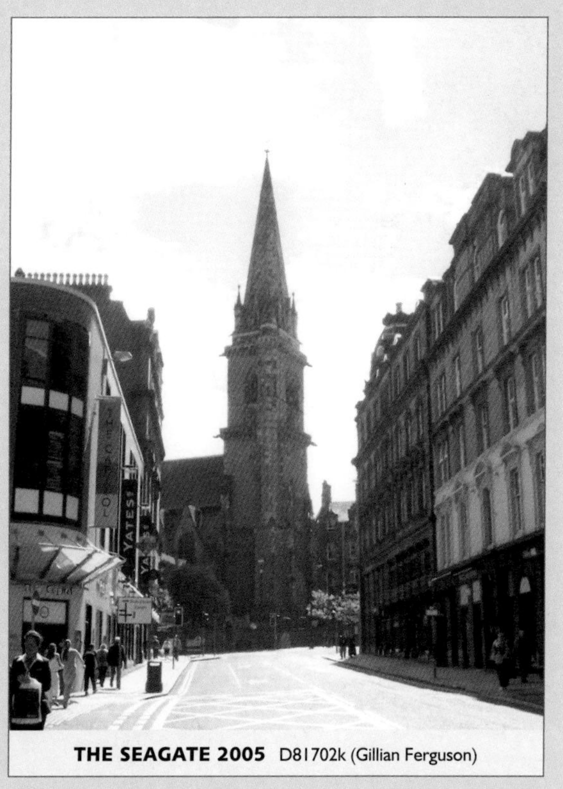

THE SEAGATE 2005 D81702k (Gillian Ferguson)

FISH STREET AND BUTCHER'S ROW c1880 ZZZ04415 (Dundee City Council, Central Library)

These attractive drawings were made by C S Lawson in about 1880, and form part of the Lamb collection in Dundee City Library. It is interesting to note the mixture of architectural styles and ages of the buildings and how cramped the streets were. The butchers and fishmongers plied their trade close to the harbour, probably near present-day Whitehall Crescent.

During the Wars of Independence in the 13th and 14th centuries, Dundee and its castle were captured and occupied by the English several times. In 1291 the English occupied the town, and in 1296 Edward I of England destroyed St Mary's Church. During this period, the castle was sacked and rebuilt several times; it may have been finally demolished by Robert the Bruce (a tactic he used all over Scotland to stop the English returning and using these strongholds). Although no detailed records of Dundee's castle exist, its memory remains in the naming of Castle Street, which runs off the present-day High Street.

Throughout this turbulent period, the inhabitants of Dundee seem to have been able to recover quickly, rebuilding their town and never ceasing in their trade with foreign ports. Indeed, throughout the 14th and 15th century Dundee was the third largest town in Scotland (behind Edinburgh and Aberdeen) in terms of both size and wealth. A downshift in the importance of the Seagate can be seen with the relocation of the tolbooth to the Marketgait (the modern-day High Street) in 1363; a tron or weighing beam was already situated here. The Seagate was still a residential area, but the commercial hub may have felt safer being located nearer to the castle's fortifications, and it made sense to be nearer the harbour. By 1400 the market cross had joined the tolbooth and relocated to the High Street.

> ## Did you know?
> **William Wallace**
> *It is said that William Wallace attended the grammar school in Dundee's High Street as a young man. A fight with a fellow pupil, Selbie, ended in murder when Wallace stabbed him. Unfortunately for Wallace, Selbie was the son of an English governor, and Wallace was forced to flee the town.*

Two churches dominated Dundee. St Clement's, near the castle, was probably the first parish church, while St Mary's in the Field, as the name suggests, was outside the more densely populated area, which gives an idea of the size of the town at the time. Only St Mary's survives, although the present-day church dates from a much later period; the Old Steeple, the oldest surviving part, was built during the 1440s. St Clement's churchyard was the main burial ground, covering the area of the present-day city square and Caird Hall, and running down to the harbour. Only the larger public buildings such as the churches would have been built of stone. Most buildings were constructed from wood, but by this date with more sophisticated timber frames. Smaller dwellings would have continued to resemble little more than shacks.

Dundee had a problem in that space for expansion was limited. To the east, off the Seagate, the Murraygate and Cowgate developed. North from the High Street the ground was swampy and unsuitable for building, so development began southwards along the Nethergate (originally a coastal path to Perth) and northwards to form the Overgate. Some larger houses kept their grounds and gardens, but behind many of them smaller dwellings and business premises started to use up the space. A labyrinth of closes and alleyways also grew between the larger buildings which faced the High Street. The street patterns that formed as Dundee began to grow are still much the same today, but few buildings from before 1700 survive, and many of the closes have been lost or have been partially swallowed up by later buildings.

Dundee was not well defended. A town wall was not built until the late 15th century, and even then the wall incorporated existing garden walls. Each road into town had a port, or gate, through which traders entering the town had to pass and pay the town's levies. As the town grew, the gates would move to new positions. Many of the ports gave their names to the areas they were situated in;

THE OLD TOWER AND THE CROSS c1880 SA000147
(Courtesy of University of St Andrews Library)

The Old Tower is referred to locally as the 'Auld Steeple'. The cross in the foreground is the Mercat (market) Cross, which dates from 1586. The cross has been moved a few yards to the left from the position in this photograph, but it was originally sited in the Seagate. Only the shaft is original; today it is topped with a modern reproduction of the unicorn.

these names are still in use today, for example West Port, Murraygate, and Cowgate. In 1770, many of the ports were removed, but Wishart Arch in the Cowgate can still be seen today. The story of Dundee's harbour is similar to that of its walls. The harbour does not seem to have been properly maintained until the 1440s, and it was not until the 16th century that a pier master was employed to be responsible for the upkeep of the harbour.

By the 16th century, Dundee was again subject to English attack and occupation. Henry VIII's troops captured Broughty Castle and built a fort high above Broughty Ferry on the area now known as Fort Hill. Broughty Castle was an excellent stronghold: it was hard to reach, as it sat across a causeway that could only be crossed at low tide. The English were in a strong position here, and regularly staged raids upon the surrounding countryside. In 1548, they sailed towards Dundee and sacked the town, burning St Mary's Church and destroying many of Dundee's archival documents from before this time. The Catholic forces of the infant Mary, Queen of Scots, led by Regent Arron, were no match for the English troops; they had also been severely hampered by outbreaks of plague. Eventually the Scots were forced to employ French and German mercenaries to help them fight the English. The English were finally forced to retreat back to Broughty Ferry. The Scots laid siege to it for nearly three years until February 1550, when the English surrendered and were allowed to leave.

Dundee's townscape had been badly damaged by the English invasion, and its inhabitants again suffered from the plague in 1585, which lasted for more than a year. Fear of the disease was so great that town meetings were held in the open air on what is today Magdalen Green rather than in the tolbooth. Once again, Dundonians were left to recover

DUDHOPE CASTLE 2005 D81703k (Gillian Ferguson)

Dating from around 1580, Dudhope Castle was the principal seat of the Scrymgeours, the hereditary constables of Dundee. By the 1750s the castle was dilapidated; it was later used as a woollen mill, and then as barracks. Today the castle exterior has been fully restored and is used as offices.

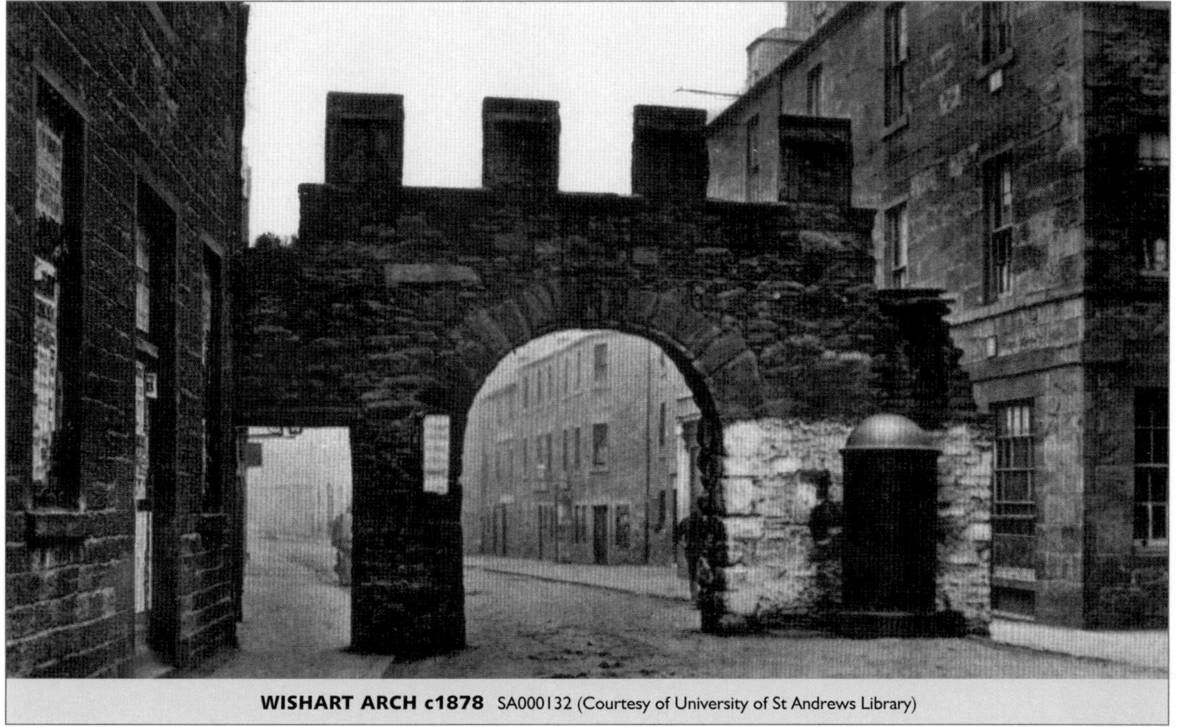

WISHART ARCH c1878 SA000132 (Courtesy of University of St Andrews Library)

Wishart Arch still stands in the Cowgate today, although the surrounding buildings have disappeared. The arch was said to have been used by the reformer George Wishart to preach to the townsfolk inside the burgh walls and to the plague victims who were forced to live outside the walls.

Did you know?

The Cost of Witch Burning

Records from 1590 give details of the cost to Dundee of hanging and burning a witch: it was over £5, a substantial amount at the time. This included the transporting of the wretched accused, the purchasing of coal, tar and rope, and the payment for the hangman.

from the devastation left by invading forces, and a period of rebuilding began. Although St Mary's church tower survived, the English had removed its bells and demolished much of the main church. The school attached to the church had also been burnt by English forces, and the tolbooth building was badly damaged. By the late 1580s, the town was recovering its prosperity; the opportunity for improvements must have been taken, as at this date many of the wooden buildings were replaced with stone and many thatched roofs replaced by slate. St Clement's Church had been falling into disrepair, and many buildings began to encroach upon its churchyard. Indeed, the church graveyard was reported to be overflowing, and the people were naturally worried that this was unsanitary. It was in 1564 that Mary, Queen of Scots visited the town and granted the townspeople the right to use the grounds of Greyfriars Monastery as a burial ground, known as the Howff. Although the monastery has long disappeared, the Howff survives as a beautiful green oasis of quiet within the city centre, situated in Meadowside. A range of interesting and illustrious gravestones, dating from between the 16th and late 19th centuries, are surrounded by high walls and railings; one wall incorporates arcading from the early 1600s.

THE HOWFF 2005 D81704k (Gillian Ferguson)

This view of the Howff shows the Meadowside aspect of D C Thomson's Courier buildings. The well-tended graveyard is a pleasant refuge in the busy city.

A HOWFF GRAVESTONE 2005 D81705k (Gillian Ferguson)

Many of the gravestones within the Howff show a high standard of carving, and some date from as early as the 16th century. There is an ongoing project to record each stone, and the stones are monitored to check their condition.

Restoration of St Mary's was also undertaken; but changes in religious thinking were taking place within Dundee even before the Reformation. Indeed, Dundee was known as 'the second Geneva' owing to its enthusiasm for the new religious ideas. The interior of St Mary's, which would have been lavishly decorated, was simplified, and pews were introduced for the first time. It was typical for important families or institutions to own the pews; for example, each trade had its own pew. The church had previously been responsible for education, and the grammar school run by the church provided a classical education for those training to become priests or state servants. The new grammar school built in 1589 was under the control of the town council rather than the church.

By the end of the 16th century, Dundee was emerging as an important trading centre, with contacts across Europe. Already its inhabitants had shown characteristic resilience and mercantile skills. Dundee's street pattern, with the Seagate, Marketgate, Cowgate and Nethergate, is still recognisable today, and the skyline of the burgh was, and still is, dominated by St Mary's tower. However, Dundee's wealth and prosperity would soon become an attractive target for invading forces.

Dundee's Nine Trades

The Nine Incorporated Trades were formed in the 16th century; the object was for members to receive a fair price for their services, to emphasise fair trade, and to discourage non-members from undercutting the price of their goods. The nine members, which were listed in order of importance, were the bakers, the cordiners (shoemakers), the glovers, the tailors, the bonnet makers, the fleshers (butchers), the hammermen (metal workers), the weavers, and the dyers. By co-operating, the different trades had strong political powers, and took an active interest in the welfare of Dundee. One of their earliest meeting places was within the Howff cemetery. Each trade held its meeting at the gravestone of one of its former members, until the Trades were able to build the Trades Hall in 1778. The Trades funded the building of St Andrew's Church in 1774, and here 'the Kirkin of the Trades' is still held every November.

ST ANDREW'S CHURCH 2005
D81706k (Gillian Ferguson)

FOREIGN & BRITISH EMPORIUM
DEALER in HARDWARE And FANCY GOODS
A BARRIE
HOUSE AGENT

HIGH STREET c1900 SA000193
(Courtesy of University of St Andrews Library)

This photograph, taken around the year 1900, shows much earlier buildings still in existence. The shops we see here include the Foreign and British Emporium, 'dealer in Hardware and Fancy Goods', and Young & Company's Dressmaking Rooms. The police officer in the centre is keeping a watchful eye!

CHAPTER TWO

A Mercantile Burgh

THROUGHOUT THE many hardships that the burgh of Dundee had faced, the burgh-dwellers were always able to rally in terms of both physically repairing the townscape and recovering economically. However, buffeted by both sides during the ensuing Civil War, Dundee was about to face some of its most difficult times, and recovery would be slow. The disputes between the King and Parliament had seen Charles I executed by Cromwell in 1649. Scotland, owing to religious divisions, was in a weakened state, and the crowning of Charles II at Scone and his recognition as King brought Scotland into conflict with the Parliamentarians.

By the end of the 16th century the population of Dundee had risen to around 10,000, and the burgh was the second most prosperous in Scotland next to Edinburgh; it traded with England, the Baltic states, the Netherlands, Norway, France and Spain. Dundee had begun to manufacture and export coarse cloth, and the records of one Dundee merchant, David Wedderburne, mentions that this was destined for the Baltic. This in turn led to a demand for hemp or flax, and is an early indicator of Dundee's textile industry. Wedderburne also lists imported goods to the town such as timber, iron, salt, syrup, vinegar and fruit. Dundee was also one of the largest importers of claret into Scotland, supplying the religious orders and the royal household.

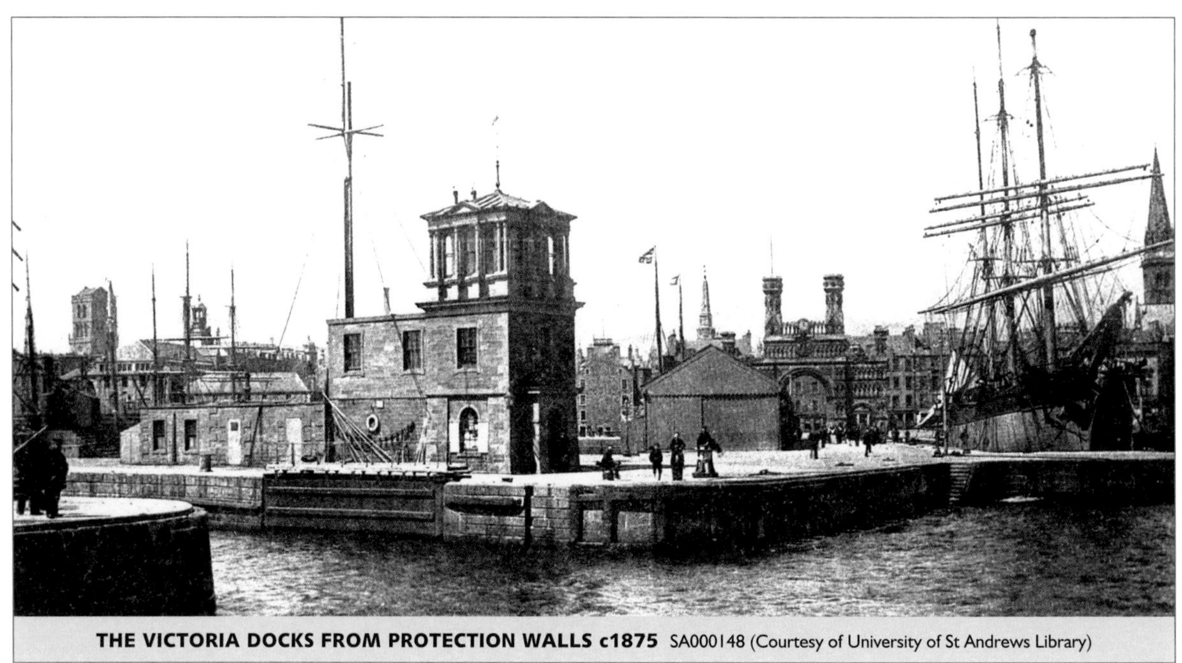

THE VICTORIA DOCKS FROM PROTECTION WALLS c1875 SA000148 (Courtesy of University of St Andrews Library)

The masted vessel to the right of the picture may be one of Dundee's many whalers. The main building in the foreground is the Dock Master's office. St Mary's tower is in the distance on the left-hand side.

Wealth, however, could not stave off the dreaded plague, which returned once again in 1605 and lasted for over four years. The authorities had tried to clean up Dundee, both physically and morally, to little avail. Refuse and animal and human waste was supposed to be dumped at sea or put in middens in the backlands of buildings, but there were still complaints that many latrines drained into paths and highways, and roaming livestock fouled the streets. Mixed with industrial waste, this effluent contaminated the water supplies. Measures were taken to counteract this; for example, lime pits were moved to the east end of the Seagate to make use of the Dens Burn, which was not used as a domestic supply. Those suffering from leprosy were kept outwith the town, near the Dens Burn, and only a small group were allowed to enter the town at specific times to purchase the goods they needed. There were now strict laws governing nearly all aspects of everyday life, with heavy punishments and fines in place should they be broken. Musicians were fined for playing after 9pm, and there was a strict 10pm curfew. A new prison was also provided for 'adulterers and fornicators'.

Dundee City Churches

The original church was built by David, Earl of Huntingdon in 1190. In 1303 Edward I, the Hammer of the Scots, destroyed the church, and it was not until the 1400s that building began on what was to become at that time the longest ecclesiastical building in Europe. St Mary's tower was completed in the 1480s; it is the only original part of the building still standing, as most of the church was destroyed by fire in 1547. A small portion of the east end of the church survived and was re-used, becoming the East Kirk, and in the 16th century the south transept was rebuilt to house another church, known as the South Kirk. In 1759 a third church was built in the north transept, the Cross Church, and in 1789 the nave was rebuilt as the Steeple Kirk. Dundee was now in the unique position of having four separate churches under one roof! Fire struck again in 1841, and only the tower and Steeple Kirk were saved. The congregation of the Cross Church moved out, but the other churches were rebuilt, and three congregations used the buildings until the 1980s.

ST MARY'S TOWER AND THE NEW OVERGATE CENTRE 2005
D81707k (Gillian Ferguson)

With the ongoing threat of civil war, the town's defences needed to be improved. Those residents whose property boundaries made up part of the wall were instructed to improve their sections; any buildings outwith the town wall were demolished, so that there were no hiding places for approaching enemies. The defences held in 1644 when the Marquis of Montrose first attacked the town, but during a second attack in 1645 Montrose gained Corbie Hill (roughly the site of present-day Lindsay Street) where the wall had been poorly built and blasted Dundee with cannons. Luckily, Covenanter troops were nearby, and Montrose spent mere hours in the town before being forced to make a hasty retreat. Another wave of plague raged through the east of Scotland in the same year, but this time the authorities were better prepared, closing the ferry service at Dundee and controlling movement in and out of the burgh. Despite these efforts, the disease struck again for the final time in 1647.

By 1651, Dundee was in a good position to withstand an attack: the defences were strong, and Governor Robert Lumsden and his troops were in situ. This air of confidence and security was undoubtedly felt by many of Dundee's smaller neighbours, who lodged their artefacts, treasures and valuables within the town for safekeeping. Unfortunately, this served to make Dundee a more attractive target for General Monck, who laid siege to the town later that same year, bombarding it from ships anchored on the Tay. Lumsden and his troops managed to hold out for nearly six weeks believing that a relief army was on the way, little knowing that they had been ambushed and captured at Alyth. Monck only became more determined to gain Dundee. When he realised that a local boy was allowed into the burgh every day to play with friends, the boy was interrogated; he revealed that the defending soldiers began drinking every day at breakfast and were drunk by lunch. Monck saw his chance and stormed the town, breaching its defences

Did you know?

Mass graves thought to contain the remains of those killed during the massacre by Monck's troops have been found around St Mary's Church. Burials have been found on three separate occasions: during the laying of tram tracks in the 19th century, whilst the Old Overgate was being demolished in the 1960s, and more recently when landscaping was being undertaken around the churches.

ST MARY'S TOWER AND THE CHURCHES
c1878 SA000143
(Courtesy of University of St Andrews Library)

on 1 September 1651. The massacre that followed saw an estimated 12,000 soldiers and townsfolk killed, including many women and children. Lumsden and a few of his men barricaded themselves in St Mary's tower until they were eventually smoked out and executed; Lumsden's head was displayed on a spike on the tower for nine years.

As a result of their victory, Monck and his New Model Army were entitled to loot captured settlements for one day; but the long siege and the large amount of booty to be found increased their lust, and a week of violent pillaging throughout the town followed. 60 ships moored in the harbour were commandeered by Monck's army and filled with plunder; but thanks to what must have been seen as divine justice, not one ship made it past the mouth of the River Tay. All mysteriously sank, and the treasures were

lost. The citizens struggled to deal with the number of dead from the massacre, and were forced to bury the dead in mass graves. To retain order, Monck took up residence in the town (near the present-day entrance to the Overgate Centre) and kept a garrison of solders. Later he was to remove the defensive walls that surrounded the town. Dundee never really regained the status that it had previously enjoyed, and its recovery was slow. Residents faced a depressing situation with the loss of wealth and buildings, and the town's population was slow to increase.

By the early 1700s, Dundee had a vast array of different trades, which in many cases interlinked and relied upon each other. Cotton and woollen cloth were still woven in the burgh, and many inhabitants were employed in the making of coloured thread, rope making, and glass making. Shoe making was another large industry, and with it went buckle making and leather tanning. Dundee had been an early manufacturer of guns, and was famed for its production of high-quality pistols. Dundee had also always been an important centre for whaling, and with this went shipbuilding. For the most part these trades were still undertaken in the centre of the town, but the Hilltown, always known for its bonnet makers, was where most of the handloom weavers lived, as here they had the water supplies they needed to boil and clean their yarns. However, all these trades were to suffer with the 1707 Parliamentary Union and the move away from the burgh system that had allowed Dundee merchants and manufactures to thrive. The 1707 Union had resulted in central government having much more control over trade; furthermore, Scotland was no longer independent, but a part of Great Britain. Thus burghs like Dundee faced heavier competition and higher taxes. Trade with the Netherlands, always important to Dundee, had collapsed, and trade with France had lessened. There was now a high demand for goods in the Americas, but Dundee struggled to compete with the ports on the west coast of Scotland, which had a distinct advantage for trans-Atlantic trading.

General Monck's Treasure

For centuries people have believed that the treasure General Monck's armies looted from Dundee is still on the seabed somewhere between Broughty Castle and Tayport. Although the water is only around 40ft deep in this area, the sandbanks and currents are notoriously treacherous. If the haul included 200,000 gold coins, as some believe, along with other precious items, it could be worth over £2 billion in today's money. In 2002 the thought of such treasure attracted a team to undertake a three-day survey of the seabed using the most advanced technology available. Unfortunately, all that was found was a 4kg solid shot cannon ball, thought to date from around the time of Monck's attack, and now on display in the McManus Galleries.

Dundee's Whaling Industry

Dundee has always been an important centre for whaling, with the industry dating back as far as the 12th century. The Dundee Whale Fishing Company was set up in 1754. By 1811 the whaling fleet consisted of ten ships, and was big enough to rival Peterhead. With the introduction of coal gas lighting, the industry began to suffer, as whale oil was no longer required to light lamps. The industry was saved as Dundee's use of jute grew: whale oil was vital to soften the raw jute. The whalers were also important for the exploration of the Arctic regions, and University College, Dundee was said to have had the best Arctic zoological collection in Britain.

REFORM STREET 2005 D81708k (Gillian Ferguson)

Reform Street was the first street to be improved after the passing of the 1825 Improvement Act. Its neo-classical design is little changed today.

REFORM STREET c1878 SA000120
(Courtesy of University of St Andrews Library)

THE TOWN HOUSE c1900 SA000116 (Courtesy of University of St Andrews Library)

DUNDEE FROM THE AIR 1955 AFA61674TL

At first Dundee struggled, not just because of its east coast location but because unification had also seen standardisation on many goods sold for export. For Dundee's linen and cloth trade, this caused a huge problem, as the cloth produced by the town was of such poor quality that it was difficult to sell, especially as linen produced in Ireland and France was of much higher quality. However, as had happened so often in the past, the entrepreneurial spirit that characterised Dundee was quick to adapt to these difficult circumstances, and by the 1720s the town was pulling itself out of a slump. Improvements in the linen trade were undertaken in Scotland by the Board of Trustees for Manufacturing, which had been set up in 1727, and bounty acts in the 1740s made the exporting of coarse linen cloth an attractive business.

Linen was gradually becoming one of the larger, more profitable, industries in Dundee as its other trades struggled to survive. Manufacturers concentrated on

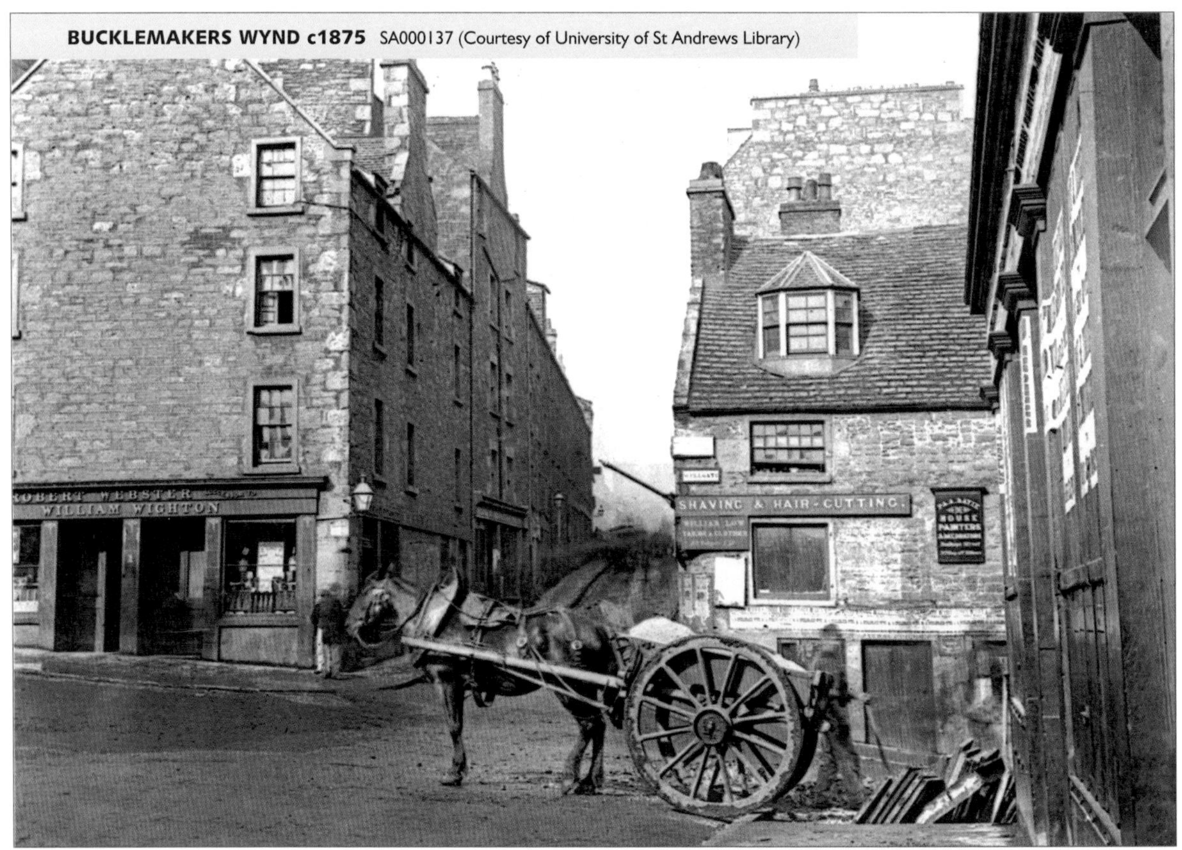

BUCKLEMAKERS WYND c1875 SA000137 (Courtesy of University of St Andrews Library)

As suggested by its name, this wynd was home to many of Dundee's buckle makers. It was located in the Wellgate area, but the wynd no longer exists, as it was swept away with the widening of Victoria Road.

making linen goods at the lower end of the market, as they knew they would not be able to compete with the more luxurious cloth coming from France and Ireland. The shoe making industry began to struggle in competition with English manufacturers, and this saw the loss of many of Dundee's tanneries; added to this, the invention of shoe laces had seen the death of the buckle making trade. The manufacture of coloured thread, however, remained important to the town well into the 1870s when nearly 3000 people were still employed in thread making in the Seagate, Wellgate and Overgate, but this industry too was in decline towards the end of the 18th century.

As a symbol of Dundee's regaining its confidence, the architect William Adam was employed to design the new Town House. Commonly known as 'the Pillars', and built in 1731, this impressive seven-bay building was thought to be one of the finest buildings in Scotland at the time. The ground floor of the building held an arcade of shops

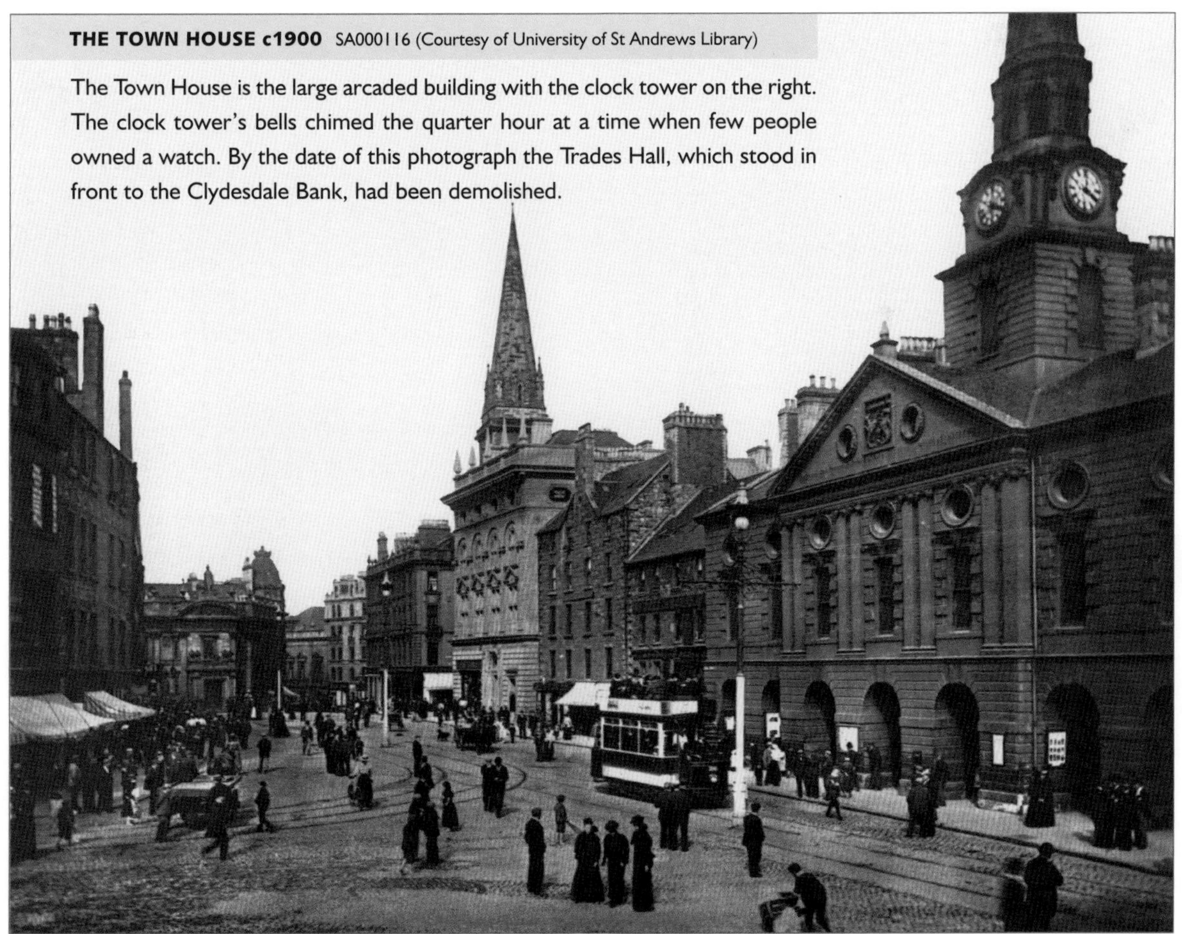

THE TOWN HOUSE c1900 SA000116 (Courtesy of University of St Andrews Library)

The Town House is the large arcaded building with the clock tower on the right. The clock tower's bells chimed the quarter hour at a time when few people owned a watch. By the date of this photograph the Trades Hall, which stood in front to the Clydesdale Bank, had been demolished.

and a bank, while above was a court, a jail and the City Chambers. The building was demolished in 1932, but its name lives on in the Pillars Bar that still trades in Crichton Street, where a model of the Town House hangs above its entrance.

The linen trade over the next 40 years was to see a six-fold increase; this was mostly due to the American Civil War of the 1760s, but as had always been the case, Dundee's lack of a running fresh water supply meant that much of the industry was situated outwith the town's boundaries. The Dighty Burn had many mills situated along its course, and such was the demand that several corn mills were converted to flax processing. Flax was shipped from the Baltic to Dundee, and sailings to Russia from Scotland increased from 12 per year in 1730 to 120 in the early 1770s. At this time Dundee still had not seen the rapid growth in industry or population that many other Scottish towns were experiencing, and it was still trade, rather than manufacturing, that was most important to the town. However, the advent of steam power would start this growth within Dundee and allow new industries to move right into the heart of the town. As was the case in much of industrial Britain, this would bring huge financial rewards for Dundee and huge improvements to the structure of the city, but at a cost to the quality of life endured by many of Dundee's inhabitants.

THE PILLARS BAR 2005 D81709k (Gillian Ferguson)

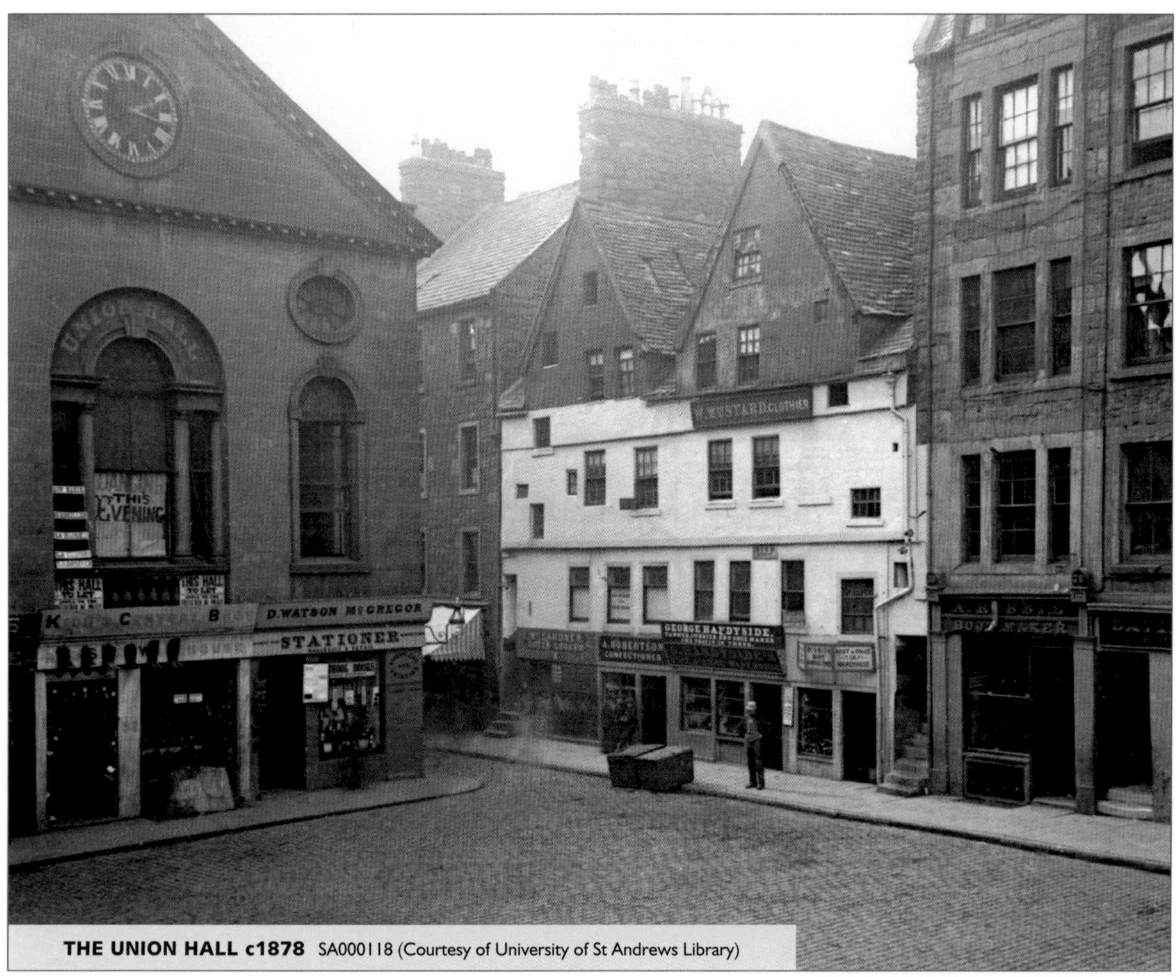

THE UNION HALL c1878 SA000118 (Courtesy of University of St Andrews Library)

The Union Hall (the building with the clock on the left-hand side) stood at the west end of the High Street (near the entrance of the present day Overgate centre). The older building in the centre of the photograph is the medieval mansion called Our Lady Warkstairs. It was the largest timber-fronted 15th-century house in Dundee. Both it and the Union Hall were demolished in 1879.

BUCKLEMAKERS WYND c1875 SA000137 (Courtesy of University of St Andrews Library)

SHAVING & HAIR-CUTTING.
HOUSE
PAINTERS

CHAPTER THREE

The Rise of Jute

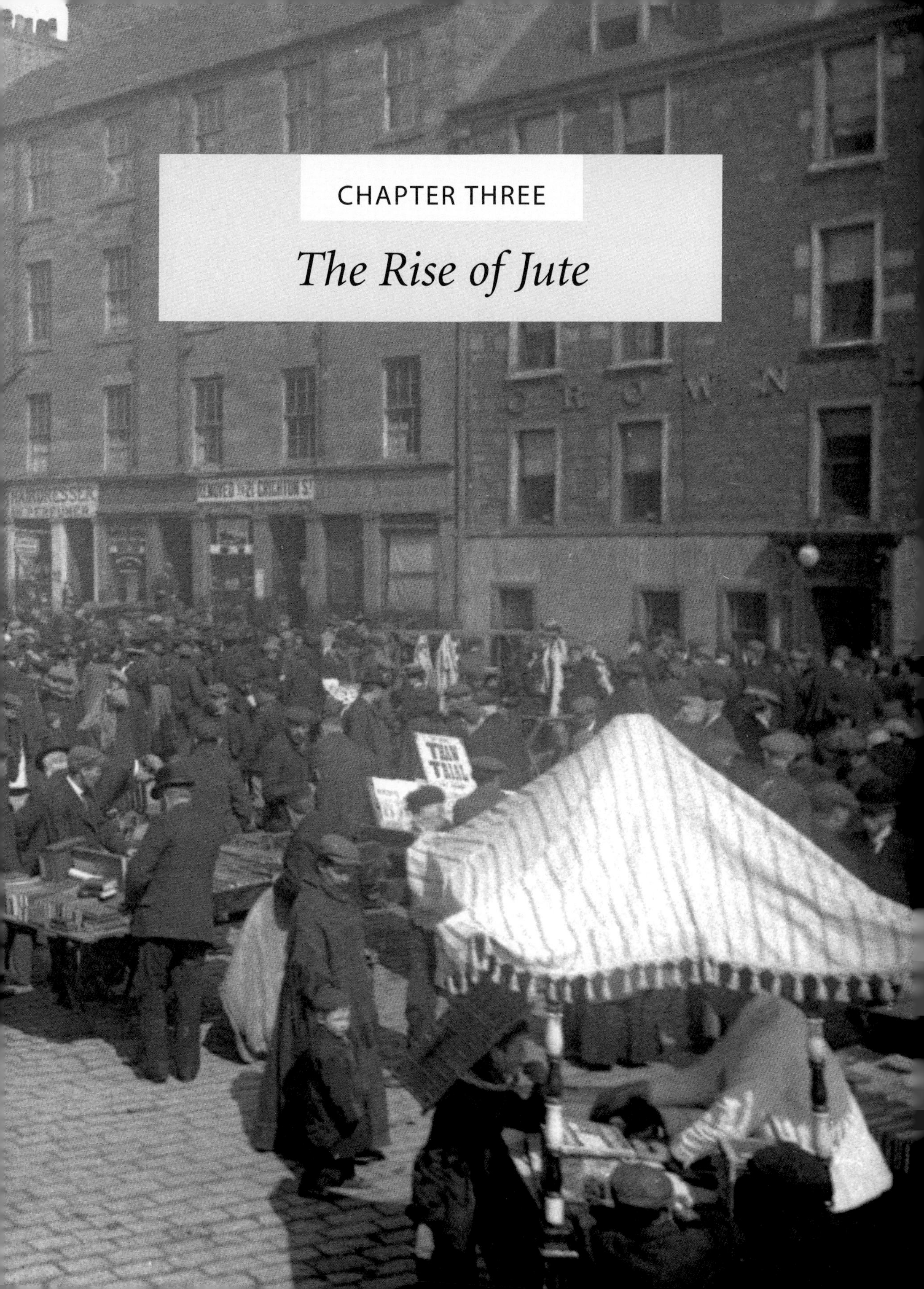

BY THE END OF THE 1700s, and at the beginning of the new century, many of Dundee's merchants saw opportunities, not just to import the raw materials needed for the production of linen but to begin to produce the goods themselves. The Napoleonic Wars saw a huge demand for sailcloth, hammocks and 'sarking' (coarse linen shirts for sailors and American slaves), and the amount of flax and hemp brought into Dundee's ports tripled. The town itself was in desperate need of improvement, being a maze of narrow, dirty, poorly planned streets. There were also problems with Dundee's harbour, which had become too full of silt and was too small to deal with the increase in the number of ships. Access to the harbour was also difficult, as the main routes were narrow and crowded. The shortage of fresh water was not only a problem for early industries within the town; there were also serious problems in supplying clean water for domestic use.

Admiral Duncan

Admiral Duncan was the son of one of Dundee's provosts, and was born in the Seagate in 1731. On 11 May 1797 Admiral Duncan encountered the Dutch fleet off the coast near the village of Camperdown. The battle that followed lasted for five hours, but the Dutch eventually surrendered to Admiral Duncan on board his ship, the 'Venerable'. This was a huge victory; Duncan, hailed a hero, was granted the title of Viscount Duncan of Camperdown. On his return to Dundee, the name of the family estate changed from Lundie to Camperdown (now Camperdown Park). A statue commemorating the hero now stands in front of Dundee's St Paul's Cathedral.

CAMPERDOWN HOUSE AND THE ADMIRAL'S TREE c1880 SA000155 (Courtesy of University of St Andrews Library)

Did you know?

Dundee aids the 'Victory'!

In the archives at Dundee University, there survives a piece of sailcloth from Nelson's 'Victory'. The sails from important ships were often cut up to make souvenirs, but this piece is particularly interesting: it bears the maker's stamp, Baxter Bros from Dundee!

The lack of a proper water supply meant that water was still collected from wells around the town or bought from the many water caddies, who could sell up to 1,000 gallons a day. Water caddying must have been a profitable business in Dundee, as many of the caddies would come from outwith the town to do business, queuing at the wells early in the morning to fill their carts. Of course, this was a perfect way for disease to spread, and there were

HIGH STREET c1870 SA000113 (Courtesy of University of St Andrews Library)

The Trades Hall at the far end of the street stood in front of the present-day Clydesdale Bank.

several outbreaks of cholera in Dundee throughout the 1800s.

In the late 18th century a Dundee that can be recognised today began to form. The town employed an architect, Samuel Bell, and his designs included many fine buildings, such as St Andrew's Church in 1772 (situated in King Street) and Provost Riddoch's Mansion in 1790 (situated between the Queen's Hotel and the DCA) in the Nethergate. Samuel Bell also designed the Trades Hall, built in 1776 and now demolished, which sat at the eastern end of the High Street in front of the Clydesdale Bank.

Attempts were also made to improve access to and from the harbour with the creation of Crichton Street in 1783 and then Castle Street in 1795. Crichton Street was named after the mansion of Dr Crichton that the council purchased and demolished to create the street. To form Castle Street the council needed to blast through solid rock. However, once they were completed both streets were still poorly paved and quite steep; although an improvement on the older wynds, they too would prove too narrow for the increasing volume of traffic. Castle Street is also the site of Dundee's first official theatre, the Theatre Royal (now the tourist information office), although only the facade survives. Also designed by Samuel Bell, the Theatre Royal opened in Dundee in 1800 with a performance of Shakespeare's 'The Merchant of Venice', perhaps the reason for the bust of Shakespeare that can still be seen on the front of the building.

A THEATRE POSTER ZZZ04416 ((Dundee City Council, Central Library)

Provost Riddoch

Andrew Riddoch became Provost of Dundee in 1787, and dominated the council for the next 30 years. Riddoch flouted the rule that the provost's position could only be held for two consecutive years by serving his own two years, making sure that someone under his control was elected for the following two years, and then again returning to serve as provost. Provost Riddoch did, however, have the difficult job of trying to modernise a town that was fast outgrowing its services, and for the most part he was very successful in doing so. Some might say, though, that many of his schemes for Dundee arose out of self-interest. For instance, Riddoch owned land that was purchased by his own council to widen streets; he also owned property around the harbour, so he would profit from the harbour improvement schemes.

Andrew Riddoch (elected Provost of Dundee in 1787) and the town council were slow to react to the problems of Dundee's harbour, but in 1815, a new Harbour Commission was formed; the task of planning the harbour was given to Thomas Telford. The new harbour took ten years to complete, and 20,000 people attended the opening of the new King William IV Dock. Like Castle Street and Crichton Street, it was soon found to be unable to cope with the increase of traffic to and from Dundee. The Earl Gray Docks, completed in 1834, Camperdown Docks (1865) and Victoria Docks (1875) were created to deal with the growing number of ships.

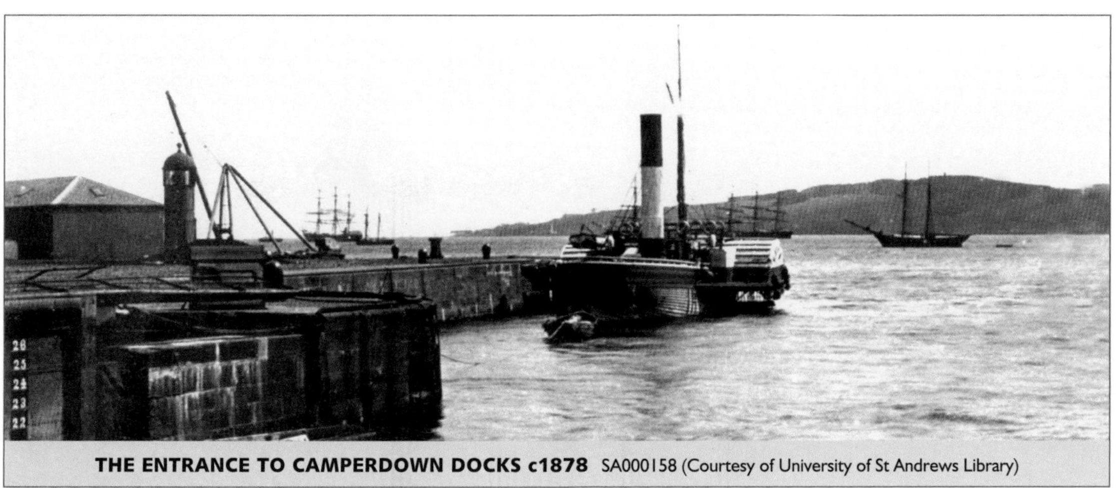

THE ENTRANCE TO CAMPERDOWN DOCKS c1878 SA000158 (Courtesy of University of St Andrews Library)

This photograph shows the entrance to Camperdown Docks. The paddle steamer was probably one of the early 'Fifies' that provided a regular service across the Tay.

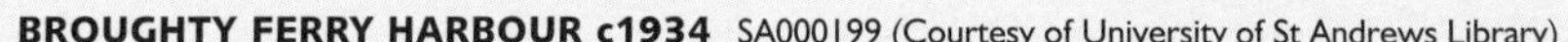

BROUGHTY FERRY HARBOUR c1934 SA000199 (Courtesy of University of St Andrews Library)

The arrival of the railway was also important for the growing town. In 1826 the Dundee & Newtyle Railway Company was formed; the line, which opened in 1832, originally terminated in Ward Road, but later extended right into the heart of the docks. This was the first railway line built in the north of Scotland. It was soon joined by the Dundee to Perth line in 1847. Dundee was also well served with railway stations, with three in the town centre: the Tay Bridge and Dundee West Station were in Union Street, and Dundee East was in Dock Street. Lochee also had its station, as did Broughty Ferry.

By the early 1800s the Napoleonic Wars had caused the market for Dundee's linen products to increase, and to keep up with the demand many of the mill owners were experimenting with new mechanical looms. At first, they struggled with the new steam technology, which could be unreliable, and new machines and parts had to be brought from places such as Leeds, which had been quicker than Dundee in embracing new technology. Those employed in hand weaving, such as the male flax hecklers, resisted the new power looms, as the wages were much lower than they were used to. (Heckling was the process of preparing flax fibres by combing and untangling, and it was traditionally a male occupation).

The new machinery that was developed to undertake this process did not require physical strength, and many of the mill owners turned to employing women, children and in some cases the infirm, as they were cheaper to employ. However, these workers were often unreliable; to try to impose discipline, many factory owners would fine workers for being late or absent, and employees could be physically punished if they did not conform. Conditions within the mills were poor, with a lack of lighting and ventilation and up to 15-hour days.

Did you know?

The Dundee & Newtyle railway line builders faced the particularly difficult problem of how to navigate the Law. Their solution was to create a quarter-mile-long tunnel through the eastern flank of the hill!

A TAY FERRY STEAMER c1905 SA000173
(Courtesy of University of St Andrews Library)

The busy 'Fifie' brings passengers back to Dundee.

Mill work was often seasonal, so many of the workers and their families would spend part of their year in the countryside, working on farms picking fruit or harvesting crops. As industry developed, a huge influx of workers moved into Dundee. The population doubled between 1750 and 1800 to over 25,000, and by 1840 had reached 60,000. The town struggled to support this huge population increase, and what we know as the city centre became overcrowded and dirty. The wealthy classes began to move to the west of the town centre to what can be thought of as Dundee's first suburb, near Magdalen Green, and, with the introduction in 1821 of a steam ferry across the Tay, to Newport. The introduction of the railway in 1841 saw the middle classes also leaving the centre of Dundee to escape the dirt and disease, and so the suburb of Broughty Ferry, once a small fishing village, was formed, and new terraces of housing were built at the foot of the Law.

At this time, few ordinary Dundonians would have travelled far from the city, but if a journey across the Tay to Fife was needed, many boats, from sailing ships to rowboats, would make the crossing for a price. There were no regular crossing times, and frequently the boat would set off only when full.

BROUGHTY FERRY HARBOUR c1930 SA000199 (Courtesy of University of St Andrews Library)

The pretty harbour of Broughty Ferry remains much the same today. The town has two beaches: the 'stony' beach (shown here), and further east along the esplanade, the 'sandy' beach.

A TAY FERRY STEAMER c1905 SA000173 (Courtesy of University of St Andrews Library)

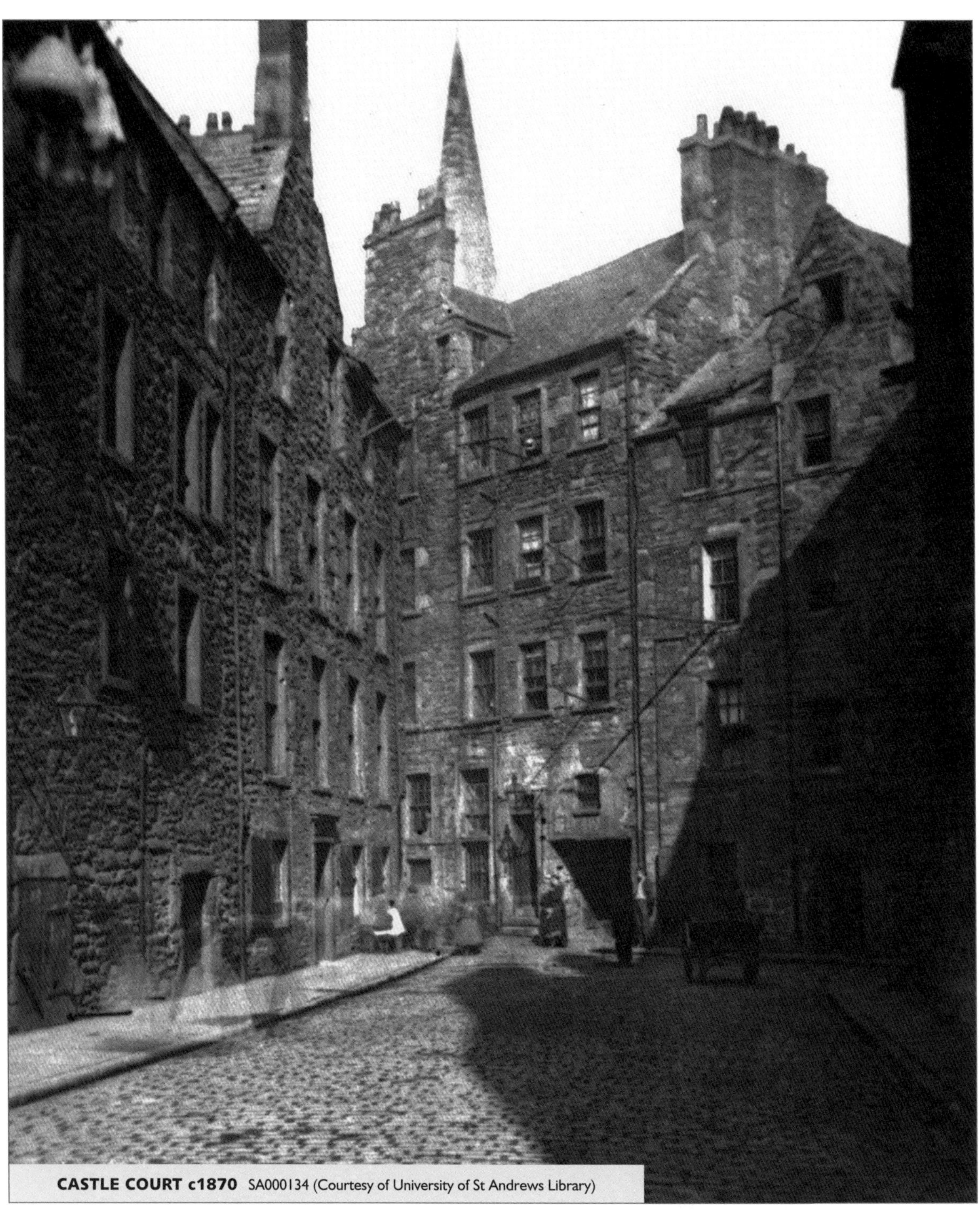

CASTLE COURT c1870 SA000134 (Courtesy of University of St Andrews Library)

Castle Court was a typical example of Dundee tenements.

The centre of town was now left to the poor, who had no choice but to live near the mills and foundries where they worked. Living conditions in town were cramped, and the larger dwellings of the wealthy, who had been able to escape, were sub-divided and shared by several families - often one entire family lived in only one room. Mills and factories and their associated buildings began to encroach right into the centre of town. With them came pollution, and Dundee's ongoing problems with the supply of adequate fresh drinking water meant that diseases such as cholera, typhus, smallpox, whooping cough and scarlet fever became rife in the first half of the 19th century. Few homes had indoor lavatories; most had basic facilities shared by several families that were little more than pits. These were emptied into the streets when full and then the waste was carted away. The Dundee Water Act of 1845 sought to alleviate these problems by piping fresh water from the Stobsmuir and Monikie reservoirs. However, this only added to the problem, as now mills could be built anywhere, and mill owners chose to build near to where workers were living. It was not until 1874 that Dundee's water supply was deemed more adequate with water piped from Lintrathen Loch and the new Clatto Reservoir. An underground sewage system piped waste into the Tay.

A gas works opened in Peep o' Day lane in 1826. The new gas lighting allowed mills to open for longer hours and so to employ even more workers. Irish immigrants began to move to Dundee in huge numbers, further swelling the population, even though the wages paid in the town were lower than in other areas of Scotland. There was relatively little new house building within Dundee, and much of what was built was of poor quality and hastily built. The houses were often damp and cold, and in some cases structurally unsafe. Some of the mill owners,

THE VAULT 1878 SA000138
(Courtesy of University of St Andrews Library)

The Vault is a good example of the narrow streets and wynds that were cleared following Dundee's Improvement Acts.

however, such as Baxter Brothers, tried to build better housing for their workers. The tenements that Baxter's built in Lyon Street were of a superior standard, with large rooms and high ceilings. They still had outdoor lavatories, but each home had its own boiler and grate at a time when many homes had no cooking facilities and food was bought from street vendors. It was not unusual to buy a hot potato for breakfast on the way to work! Generally, Dundee's slums were among the worst in Britain, and were regarded as being as dreadful as those in London or Glasgow.

Improvement Acts were passed in Dundee in the 1870s and embodied twenty different schemes aimed at tackling some of the town's most serious problems. New housing for the working class began to be built in all directions from the town centre to Hawkhill, along the Blackness Road, to the Hilltown, Clepington, Stobswell, and along Dens Road, but this new building was in no way planned. New housing consisted mainly of tenements, usually four storeys high, and accessed from the rear balcony or 'pletty', or from common doorways or 'closes'. Usually comprising just one or two large rooms with a range for cooking and heating, most flats shared a lavatory on each landing.

For washing purposes most people visited a public bathhouse. The ones that opened in Lochee in 1894 also incorporated a library. Some tenements had communal brick washhouses in the 'back land' or 'back green' (the back garden, usually just a square of grass) where laundry was boiled in a copper boiler with a wringer attached and then put through a mangle. Washing was then hung from 'greenie poles', or in some cases a pulley system out of the kitchen window. For those without such facilities, laundry could be done at the 'washie' (the public washhouse). For a small sum, the laundry amenities could be used, and there was the added advantage of hot air clothes driers. Even those with the facilities to do their own washing often used the washie, definitely a woman's domain and a great place to catch up on 'aw the jen' (gossip), and it was a familiar sight to see women pushing an old pram with the washing in a basket or round tin bath inside.

Flax spinning was soon to disappear in Dundee and be replaced by jute, the first of the

THE SINDERINS 1903 SA000175 (Courtesy of University of St Andrews Library)

This view has changed little over the years. It shows the junction of Hawkhill (on the left), Blackness Avenue, and Perth Road (on the right), and looks towards the city centre. The tall building in the distance is Hawkhill School, built in 1892. The tram ran from the centre to Ninewells.

three Js which made Dundee famous (the other two are jam and journalism). Jute would become the industry upon which Dundee's economy would be almost wholly dependant. The 1870s saw the peak of the linen market, and foreign competition become more intense. The Crimean War had created problems with the supply of flax (three-quarters of Dundee's flax was imported from Russia), and the market for linen products in France and Germany had disappeared. Jute was seen to be an answer: the raw material was cheap, and in ready supply from India. There had been experiments in spinning jute from the early 1800s, but jute was difficult to work with, and the fabric produced was weak. It was later found that if processed properly, jute could be made into a strong and durable fabric. To process jute involved soaking the fibres with water and whale oil to make it softer and easier to spin.

THE PUBLIC BATHS c1880 SA000180
(Courtesy of University of St Andrews Library)

The public baths at West Protection Wall were the first to open in Dundee (they opened in 1848, and were improved after 1871) and incorporated Turkish baths and swimming pools.

Did you know?

William McGonagall

The poet William Topaz McGonagall (1825-1902), universally regarded as one of the worst poets ever, claimed Dundee as his adopted home. The self-educated loom weaver claimed that the Goddess of Poetry visited him in Paton's Lane in 1877, and he once walked the 50 miles to Balmoral to visit Queen Victoria. Having been stopped at the gate, he was told never to come back. His travels took him to London and even New York, where he had to rely on a Dundee benefactor to fund his trip home.

Oh, Bonnie Dundee! I will sing in thy praise
A few but true simple lays,
Regarding some of your beauties of the present day
And virtually speaking, there's none
can them gainsay;
There's no other town I know of with
you can compare
For spinning mills and lasses fair,
And for stately buildings there's none can excell
The beautiful Albert Institute or the Queen's Hotel,
For it is most handsome to be seen,
Where accomodation can be had for Duke,
Lord or Queen,
And the four pillars of the front are made
of Aberdeen granite, very fine,
And most beautiful does shine,
just like a looking glass,
And your fine shops in Reform Street,
Very few can with them compete
For superfine goods, there's none can excel,
From Inverness to Clerkenwell.
And your Tramways, I must confess,
That they have proved a complete success,
Which I am right glad to see ...

Continuing conflicts in America and the expansion of worldwide trading saw another rise in demand for the products made in Dundee. Jute canvas was used for tents and wagon covers, as sacking for coal and grain, and for horses' nosebags, among many other products. Tents from Dundee could be found in such faraway places such as America and Australia, where they were used by the gold-diggers, and Dundee's jute tarpaulins covered the pioneers' wagons as they travelled through America. As a result, rather than invest the profits from the boom in jute within Dundee, much of it was invested abroad, especially in America. Money from Dundee helped to establish and build the railroads in the US, and Dundee jute merchants invested in cattle and ranching.

Did you know?

The Postage Stamp invented in Dundee

The postage stamp was first suggested by a Dundee bookseller, James Chalmers, in 1822 (a full year before Sir Rowland Hill was officially credited with its invention). Chalmers's idea of a low-cost postage stamp was the basis of our present mailing system. Chalmers died in 1853 aged 71, and his gravestone can be found in Dundee's Howff.

The Collapse of the Tay Bridge

One of the worst disasters to affect the city was the collapse of the rail bridge in December 1879. The bridge was opened in May 1878, and at over two miles long was celebrated as the longest bridge in the world. Designed by Sir Thomas Bouch, it cost over £300,000 to build, and was viewed as one of the jewels of the modern industrial world. On the stormy evening of 28 December 1879, the centre of the bridge collapsed while a train was crossing, and 75 people fell to their death. It was later surmised that the collapse was due to a number of serious structural faults, and the disaster left Bouch a broken man. A new rail bridge, constructed close to the remains of the old one, was finally opened in 1887. The piers of the original bridge can still be seen in the river beside the main bridge - a poignant memorial to the night of the great gale of 1879.

THE TAY BRIDGE FROM THE FIFE SIDE 1880 SA000105 (Courtesy of University of St Andrews Library)

THE TAY BRIDGE, THE OLD AND NEW PIERS 1887 SA000109
(Courtesy of University of St Andrews Library)

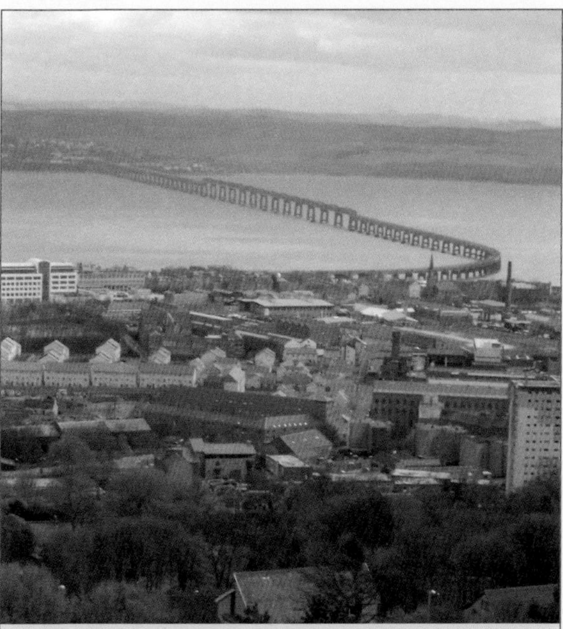

A VIEW OF THE BRIDGE FROM THE LAW 2005
D81710k (Gillian Ferguson)

It is important to remember the unique role that women played within Dundee's jute industry. Dundee earned the name of 'She-Toon' because, unlike many other places at the time, so many women were employed within the factories. Society at the time felt that the woman's place was in the home. When a woman married she was often expected to give up work, yet in Dundee a large percentage of the workforce was not only female, but also married. It was often difficult for men to find permanent work within the mills, and many young boys would become unemployed upon completing their apprenticeships, as they would then have been entitled to adult male rates of pay. With women out at work, many of Dundee's families experienced a role reversal: the men became 'kettle-bilers' (kettle boilers), so called because they stayed at home to look after the household chores and children.

Dundee's working women were known to be strong-willed and loud, and some thought them coarse – they drank and snorted snuff to clear their noses of the jute dust. The women also developed their own sign language in the mills and were able to communicate over the din of the machinery, often to the annoyance of their male supervisors, who did not understand this silent language. There was a certain hierarchy within the women working in the mills, and the job of weaving was thought of as highly superior to spinning. Weaving was certainly a cleaner job with better wages, and weavers could afford to buy luxuries like hats and gloves. Often the weavers aimed at marrying well, and stopped working once they did. Weaving was not, however, a more skilled occupation than spinning, but more responsibility was involved, because the weavers completed the end product in a long process, and any mistakes were costly. The lowest and most poorly paid class of workers sewed jute sacks, an occupation undertaken at home where, in good weather, these women could be seen sewing in their doorways. Dundee had a high proportion of unmarried women, and as they were often able to earn their own keep, many women did not marry until much later than their contemporaries in other Scottish towns.

Children made up a large part of Dundee's textile industries workforce. Many were employed as 'half-timers', spending part of

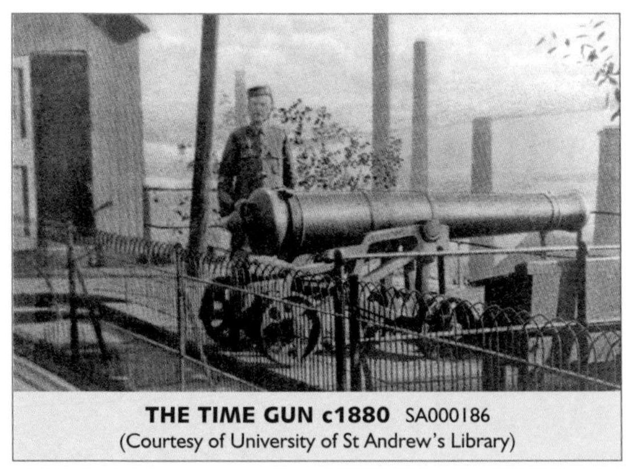

THE TIME GUN c1880 SA000186
(Courtesy of University of St Andrew's Library)

The time gun was located on a platform built into an embankment immediately to the south of Dudhope Castle. It was normally fired daily at 1pm, but it was silenced in 1916 so as not to disturb shell-shocked soldiers recovering in Dundee Royal Infirmary. The factory and foundry chimneys in the background give a sense of the density of the industrial buildings surrounding the city centre.

the day working and part of the day in school. A large number of children also had jobs delivering milk early in the morning or selling goods on the streets. For much longer than other cities in Britain, the Dundee School Board permitted children to work. In 1833, for example, the minimum age for working children was nine years old and the working day was not to exceed eight hours; however, many births were not registered, and it was difficult to prove a child's age. By 1872, school attendance was compulsory, but exemptions were made for half timers. As late as 1892 children as young as eight were still working in the mills, and even by 1900 there were still as many as 5,000 children working in Dundee. Indeed, the half-time system was not abolished until 1936. For children between the ages of 13 and 14, known as 'whole-timers', a five-day week, working from 6am to 6pm, was permitted, with the Dundee School Board insisting that they attend school between 7.15 and 9.15 pm. Although the half-timers were supposed to be gaining an education of sorts, they were often expected to attend school late in the afternoon or early evening; consequently many children were too tired to concentrate or did not attend school, and teachers often complained that classes were inattentive.

The textile industry went through many difficult periods of boom and bust, and some businesses did not succeed. Some, however, became names that are still well remembered by Dundee folk today. Cox Brothers, established in 1841, were initially situated in Foggylea before moving to their new premises in Camperdown Works. The company was the largest in the country, employing 5,000 people at its peak in 1851.

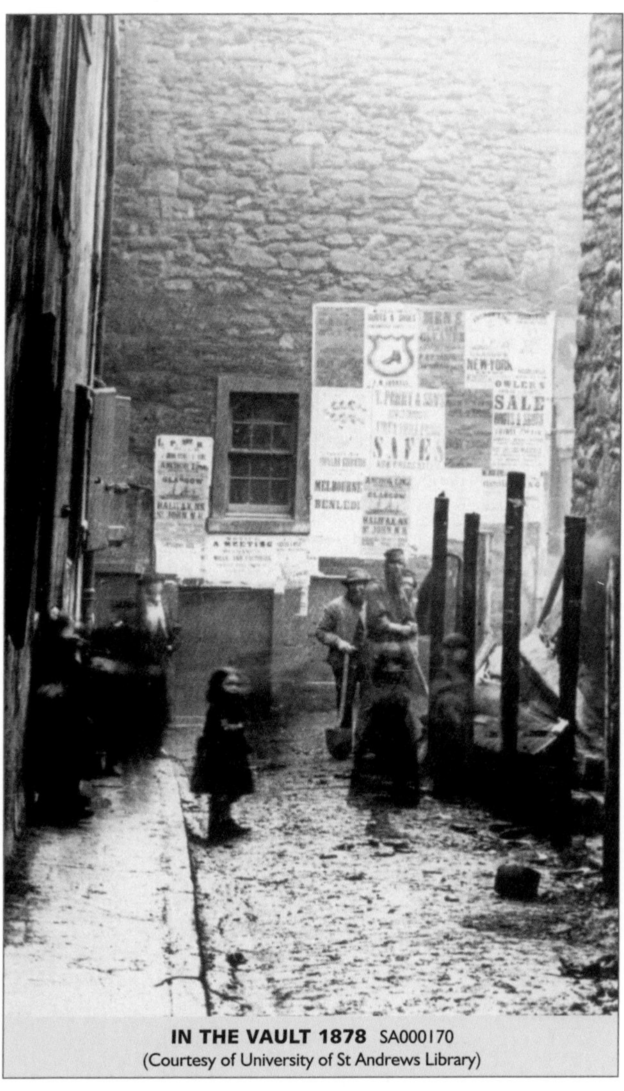

IN THE VAULT 1878 SA000170
(Courtesy of University of St Andrews Library)

The Vault was one of Dundee's most notorious slums.

Camperdown Works and the success of Cox Brothers tripled the population of Lochee, which had been a small rural village until the arrival of the railway; it officially became part of Dundee in 1859.

Camperdown Works covered 35 acres, and the High Mill is one tenth of a mile long. Cox's Stack, built in 1865, is 280 feet high; it is still a prominent Lochee landmark, and one of the few mill chimneys still to be seen in Dundee. Other well-known names within the jute industry were Gilroy & Sons, who owned the Tay Bridge Works; Grimond's, established in Dundee in the 1840s, who owned Bowbridge Works; Harry Walker & Sons with Dura and Caldrun works; and the Caird family, who owned Ashton works.

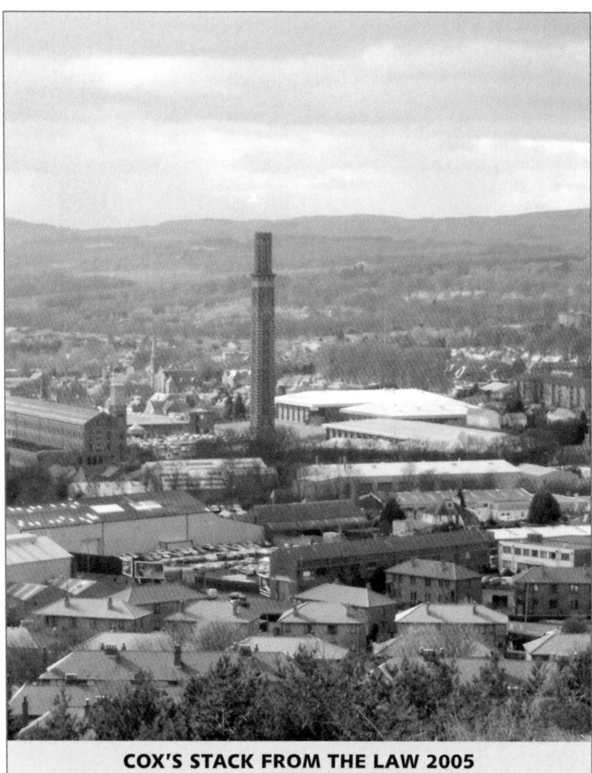

COX'S STACK FROM THE LAW 2005
D81711k (Gillian Ferguson)

Cox's Stack still dominates Dundee's skyline today. Not only was the chimney built as a status symbol, but also its height helped to keep the air cleaner at ground level.

Many of Dundee's mill owners tried to improve conditions both within their mills and within the town for the benefit of the populace as a whole. One example is the Baxter family, who were thought of as good employers by many of their workers, despite the fact that they paid slightly lower wages than some of the other mills. The work at Baxter's was much steadier than in most mills, and while there were times of high unemployment, Baxter's government contracts meant they were able to keep their core workforce. Baxter's had employed Peter Carmichael, a trained engineer, as a manager, and he had been innovative in designing both new machinery and new mills. In many of his designs for new buildings, Carmichael tried to improve ventilation and give the workforce plenty of natural light, as he felt this beneficial to the workers' health. The Baxters also provided a school, at first within rooms in Dens Street, and later at a purpose-built school in Crescent Street.

Like many of the rich textile families in Dundee, the Baxter family were also important patrons within Dundee. Always interested in education, in 1840 they provided funds for the establishment of the Watt Institute in Constitution Street where tradesmen could attend lectures to improve their education. Sir David Baxter also left £20,000 in his will to establish a Technical Institute. He was also to fund the building of the Albert Institution in 1867, now the McManus Galleries, built originally as a reference library. The building was designed by George Gilbert Scott, and was known as 'the grandest Albert Memorial outside London'. Another gift to the city's educational facilities was left by Miss Mary Ann Baxter, who willed £130,000 towards a university college - this formed the basis for the present-day university.

HILL STREET SCHOOL c1900 SA000190
(Courtesy of University of St Andrews Library)

It was probably a great novelty to see a photographer at break time!

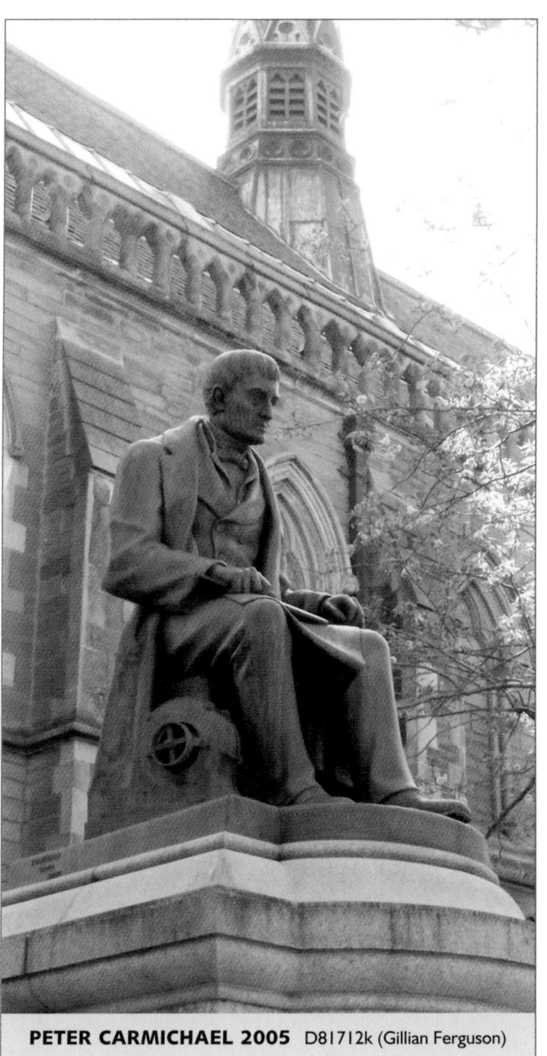

PETER CARMICHAEL 2005 D81712k (Gillian Ferguson)

THE McMANUS GALLERIES 2005 D81713k (Gillian Ferguson)

The area around the galleries is due to be modernised in the next few years. The statue seen here is of Robert Burns.

There was a new feeling of civic pride within Dundee, and these sentiments, along with the Improvement Acts, brought about attempts to enhance the town and encouraged its residents to partake in self-improvement. The centre of Dundee had a severe lack of green open spaces until 1863, when Sir David Baxter and his sisters gifted the splendid Baxter Park to Dundee. The park was opened by the Prime Minister Earl Russell, and the ceremony was attended by a huge crowd of over 60,000 people. Another popular park was Magdalen Green, created in the 1840s under the direction of Provost Alexander Lawson to create employment during a slump in the town. With views of the railway bridge and across the Tay, the park now sits much farther from the water owing to land reclamation. The bandstand was added in 1890, and concerts are still held there on Sundays throughout the summer. Balgay Hill was purchased for the town in 1871, and the Law, Dudhope Park and Lochee Park were all opened to the public over the next 20 years.

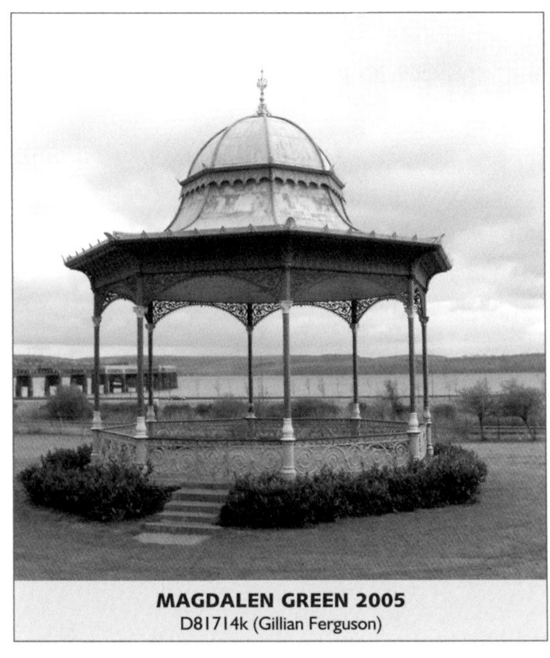

MAGDALEN GREEN 2005
D81714k (Gillian Ferguson)

THE ENTRANCE TO BALGAY PARK 1878 SA000144 (Courtesy of University of St Andrews Library)

To replace the old hospital in King Street, Dundee Royal Infirmary was built in 1853 high above the town in Constitution Road, and in 1874 Liff Hospital was provided for psychiatric treatment. Both have now closed, and will be converted into luxury flats, with new houses being built within the grounds. The Education Act (Scotland) of 1882 saw a need for better provision of secondary schooling. The High School in Dundee was the only secondary school within the town and was run as a private school, as it is today. £10,000 was gifted to the town in 1885 to create Harris Academy, which could accommodate over 1,000 pupils. However, the low fees meant that the Harris was soon suffering from a lack of places, and another school had to be found. The Morgan Hospital had been opened in 1868 as a boarding school for the sons of tradesmen, but in 1889 it became Morgan Academy with places for 650 pupils.

DUNDEE ROYAL INFIRMARY c1865 SA000115
(Courtesy of University of St Andrews Library)

Today this view no longer exists, as Dundee College's Constitution Road Campus now sits in the empty ground in front of the hospital.

MORGAN ACADEMY 2005 D81715k (Gillian Ferguson)

DUNDEE ROYAL INFIRMARY c1865 SA000115 (Courtesy of University of St Andrews Library)

Morgan Academy suffered a serious fire in March 2001, which was visible across the city. The fire was so great that at first it was feared the building could not be saved. Owing to the strong feelings of the local community that the building should be restored, a programme of conservation was undertaken. The project was completed in time for pupils returning for the 2004/05 term. Although the building's exterior has been returned to its former glory, much of the interior did not survive; the school has thus been given the chance to create a space which fits the modern needs of its pupils.

The Improvement Acts were to drastically change the centre of Dundee, beginning a period of slum clearance that would transform the medieval core of the city. A process of improvements to many of the main streets saw areas such as the Seagate, Murraygate and Commercial Street widened. Bucklemakers Wynd became Victoria Road, and Whitehall Street and Whitehall Crescent were formed. This gave Dundee the layout that can be seen today, and most of the buildings in the city centre were built after these improvements. Most of the wynds and closes disappeared, although fragments still survive between subsequent building, and practically all of the medieval buildings were demolished. One of the few survivors is Gardyne's Land, hidden behind more recent buildings in the High Street.

The buildings on the right, at the corner of Seagate and Commercial Street, have been demolished during the process of widening Commercial Street. To the left is the Clydesdale Bank; the Law can be seen in the distance.

COMMERCIAL STREET FROM BURNHEAD c1880 SA000185
(Courtesy of University of St Andrews Library)

SEAGATE LOOKING EAST FROM COMMERCIAL STREET c1900 SA000196 (Courtesy of University of St Andrews Library)

To the right, the area of empty ground seen in photograph SA000185 (see page 69) has now been built on; the scene has changed little today (the public bar on the left still survives). Before this redevelopment, many of the streets were so narrow that it was impossible for two carts to pass one another.

WHITEHALL STREET c1900 SA000119
(Courtesy of University of St Andrews Library)

This scene shows the newly created Whitehall Street with Draffen's Department Store on the left. At the end of the street the old Overgate still survives, providing a clear contrast between the new, wide, uniform streets and the old, haphazard buildings and narrow wynds and closes.

One huge change for the citizens of Dundee by the end of the 19th century was an increase in the amount of free time available for leisure pursuits. The Factory Act of Scotland meant that Saturday had become a half day for Scottish workers, and gradually the number of hours that could be worked were limited. There were also more public holidays; although these were unpaid, many saved what little they could all year so that they could enjoy these days off. Most Dundonians were still unable to afford long holidays, but day trips on public holidays were popular. Rail fares were relatively low, and a popular day out was a trip to Broughty Ferry beach or a little further along the line to Monifeith.

Another popular trip was across the Tay by either ferry or rail to Newport, and there were steamer trips along the Tay to Newburgh and Perth.

The first cycling clubs were formed in Dundee in the 1880s, and Sunday runs into the countryside were popular. Watching football became a favourite way for working men to spend a Saturday afternoon. The game was first played at West Craigie Park by Our Boys Club, formed in 1877, which would later become Dundee FC and move to Dens Park in 1899. One form of free entertainment was promenading in local parks, along the esplanade at Broughty Ferry, or simply past the shops and street vendors. This pastime was especially popular with young men and women on a Saturday evening and Sunday.

The Greenmarket was a popular area of the town centre. The traditional Lady Mary Fairs of Dundee and a weekly market were held in the Greenmarket until it disappeared with the building of the Caird Hall. The Greenmarket was described by a W J Smith in 1873 as 'greatly frequented on Saturday evenings, the attractions being of an extremely varied and diverse character ... the street preacher addressing the crowd, the quack doctor vending his nostrums, the cheap John

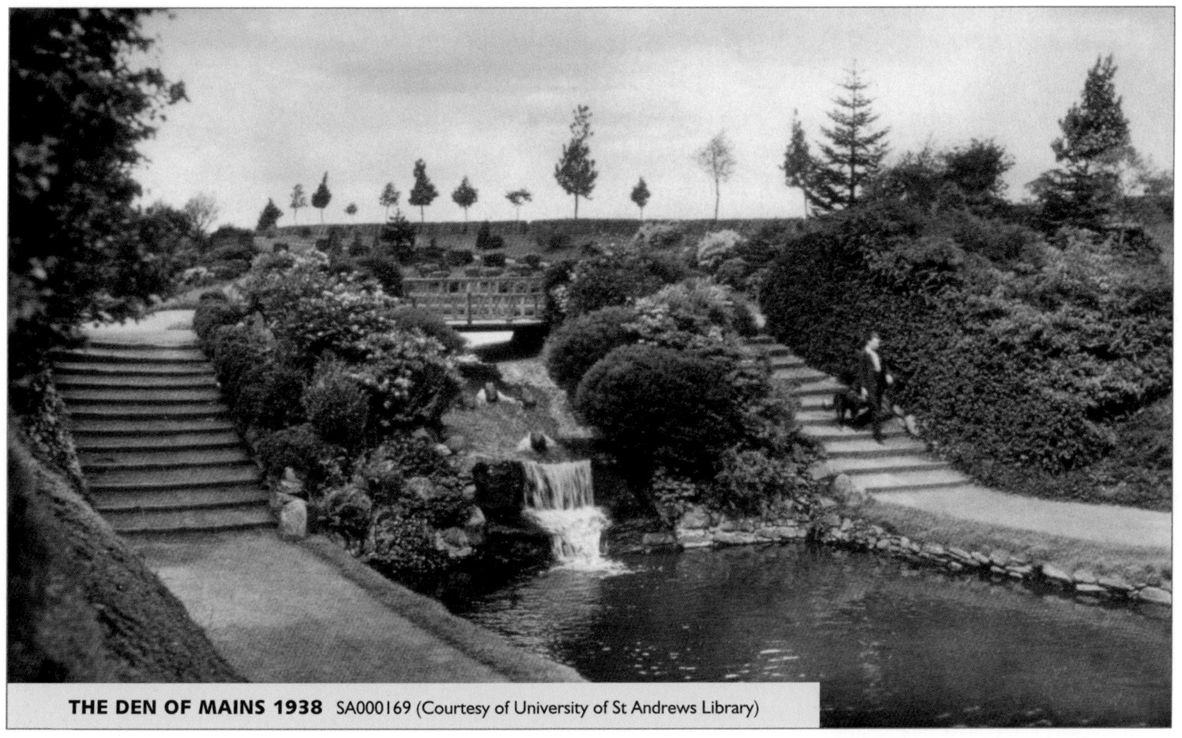

THE DEN OF MAINS 1938 SA000169 (Courtesy of University of St Andrews Library)

The Den of Mains, near Mains Castle, was a popular spot for a day out and a picnic. Only the brave frequent the area at night, as it is reputedly haunted by several ghosts!

William Bury

Dundee's last execution by hanging was carried out on 24 April 1889. William Henry Bury strangled his wife, stabbed her viciously, and then kept her body in a box (which his friends unknowingly played cards upon) for several days before confessing to the crime. It is intriguing that Bury had only recently moved to a house in Dundee's Princes Street from the Whitechapel area of London, the notorious haunt of Jack the Ripper; many people believe that Bury may have been Jack himself, as the Ripper murders stopped with his death.

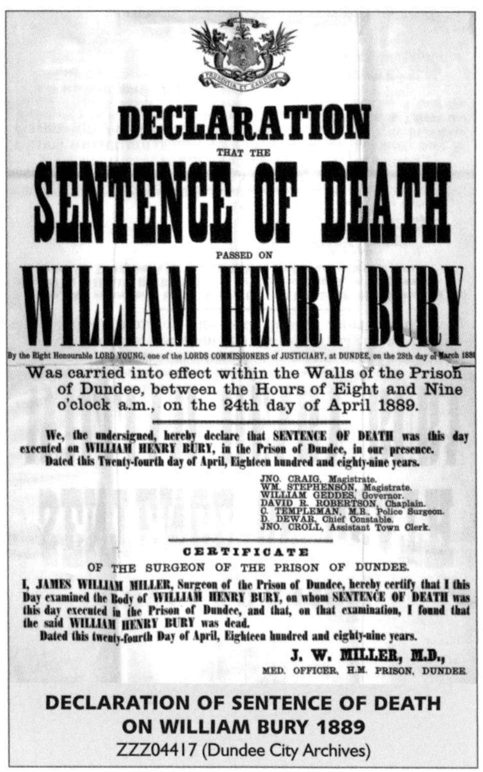

DECLARATION
THAT THE
SENTENCE OF DEATH
PASSED ON
WILLIAM HENRY BURY

By the Right Honourable LORD YOUNG, one of the LORDS COMMISSIONERS of JUSTICIARY, at DUNDEE, on the 28th day of March 188

Was carried into effect within the Walls of the Prison of Dundee, between the Hours of Eight and Nine o'clock a.m., on the 24th day of April 1889.

We, the undersigned, hereby declare that SENTENCE OF DEATH was this day executed on WILLIAM HENRY BURY, in the Prison of Dundee, in our presence.
Dated this Twenty-fourth day of April, Eighteen hundred and eighty-nine years.

JNO. CRAIG, Magistrate.
WM. STEPHENSON, Magistrate.
WILLIAM GEDDES, Governor.
DAVID R. ROBERTSON, Chaplain.
C. TEMPLEMAN, M.B., Police Surgeon.
D. DEWAR, Chief Constable.
JNO. CROLL, Assistant Town Clerk.

CERTIFICATE
OF THE SURGEON OF THE PRISON OF DUNDEE.

I, JAMES WILLIAM MILLER, Surgeon of the Prison of Dundee, hereby certify that I this Day examined the Body of WILLIAM HENRY BURY, on whom SENTENCE OF DEATH was this day executed in the Prison of Dundee, and that, on that examination, I found that the said WILLIAM HENRY BURY was dead.
Dated this twenty-fourth Day of April, Eighteen hundred and eighty-nine years.

J. W. MILLER, M.D.,
MED. OFFICER, H.M. PRISON, DUNDEE.

DECLARATION OF SENTENCE OF DEATH ON WILLIAM BURY 1889
ZZZ04417 (Dundee City Archives)

and the ballad singer, galvanic batteries, beef and sweetie stands, and exhibitions of dead and living wonders, forming altogether a curious medley.' Many shops and stalls stayed open until nine in the evening to catch this passing trade, and on a Saturday night, many stayed open until the public houses closed to catch business from those returning home.

Travelling shows and circuses were always popular, and in 1870 a wooden amphitheatre in Dock Street, which had been used by Sangers circus, was transformed into the Alhambra Music Hall. Its productions included a pantomime of Little Red Riding Hood and Hamilton's diorama, which featured large paintings being rolled across the stage to a musical accompaniment. The Alhambra was forced to close owing to structural problems - it was thought to be a danger to the public - and the owner bought a large site in the Seagate to build a new theatre. This was to become Her Majesty's Theatre and Opera House, opened in 1885 with seating for 1600 people. The opulent interior featured a marble staircase, ten boxes and gilded plasterwork.

Moving pictures could often be seen at travelling fairs and in the music halls, and these would ultimately become more popular than the live performances. By 1919 Her Majesty's Theatre and Opera House had become Her Majesty's Picture Theatre, and in the 1930s it was renamed the Majestic. Unfortunately, it was destroyed by fire in 1941. The site was redeveloped in 1956 into the Capitol

Cinema, which was still in use as a cinema until the late 1990s, when it was converted into a public house. A circus was also converted into a music hall in Lochee Road in 1891 and in the Nethergate at the Palace, where the young Harry Lauder was booed off stage. There was also the Gaiety Theatre of Varieties in Victoria Road, the Empire in Rosebank Street in the Hilltown and the King's Theatre in the Cowgate.

Like many inhabitants of industrial towns, the people of Dundee worked hard, but they also enjoyed their time off. Factory work was dirty work with long hours, and any entertainment was positively eagerly anticipated. As the town moved into the 20th century, its growth and reliance on jute as an industry in an ever-changing world meant that Dundee would encounter new problems and challenges.

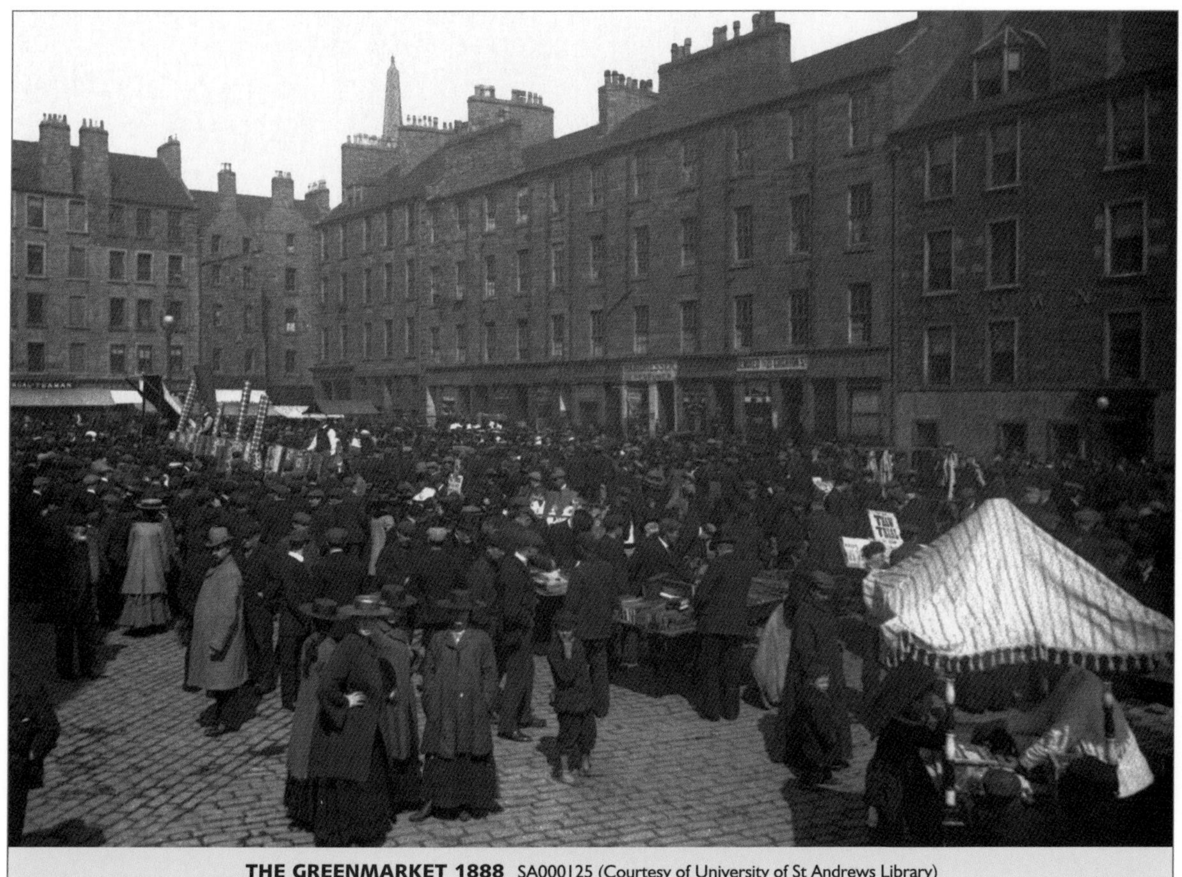

THE GREENMARKET 1888 SA000125 (Courtesy of University of St Andrews Library)

The stall with the fringed canopy seems to be selling ice cream, probably first made in Dundee by Italians. Other stalls sell rolls of linoleum and second-hand books, amongst other items. It is typical for this time that the young boy in the front of the crowd has no shoes.

THE DEN OF MAINS 1938 SA000169 (Courtesy of University of St Andrews Library)

WHITEHALL STREET c1900 SA000119 (Courtesy of University of St Andrews Library)

DINING
ROOMS
Cycle & Motor Car Agent
Cycles
Accessories
Repairs

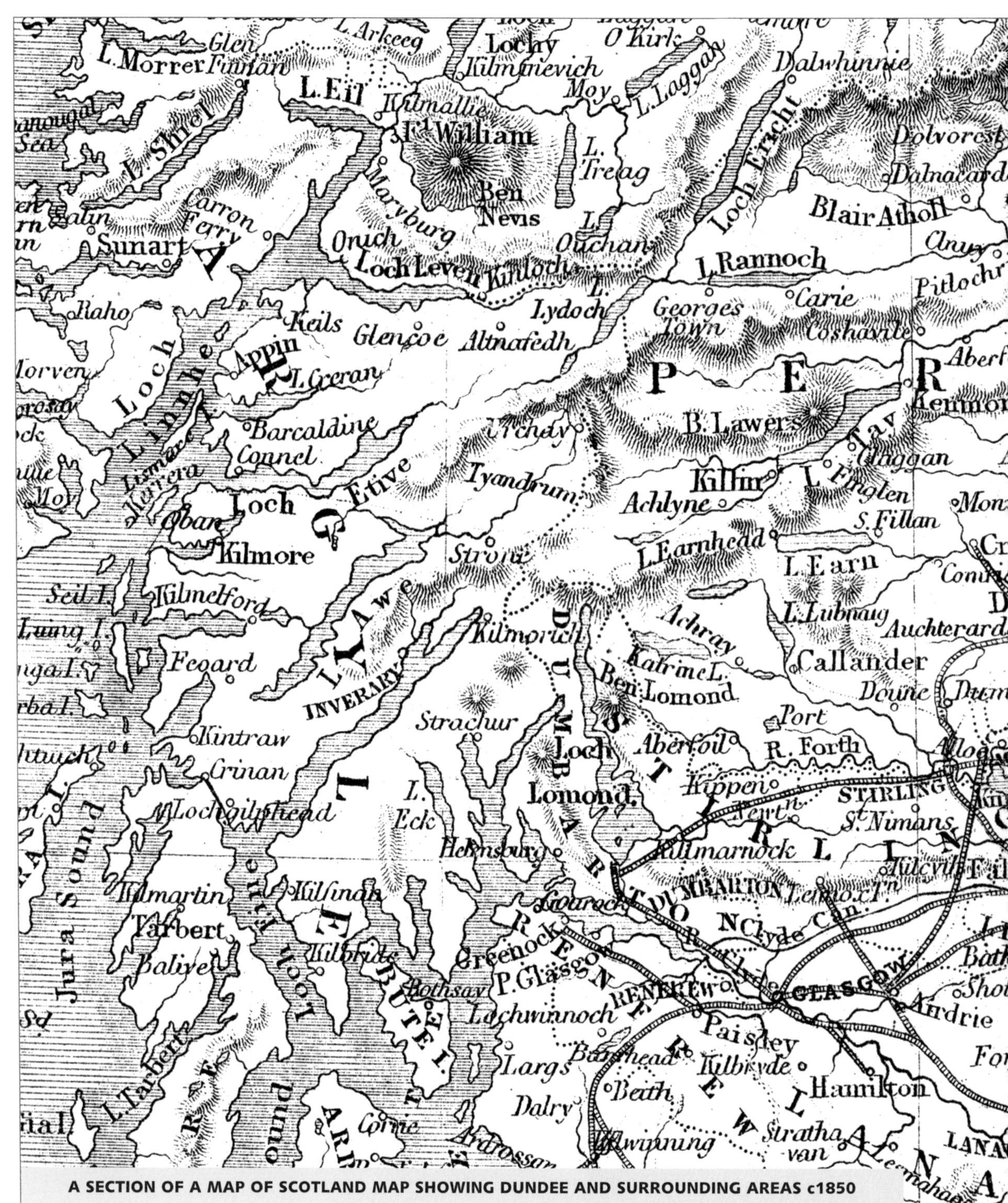

A SECTION OF A MAP OF SCOTLAND MAP SHOWING DUNDEE AND SURROUNDING AREAS c1850

Midtown
Fordon
Greenburn
Inver Bervie
Kilbo
Clova
Stricathrow
Lawrencekirk
Logie
St. Cyrus
Dun
Montrose
F O R F A
Tannadyce
S. Esk
Brechin
Glenisla
Kerriemuir
Kinnell
Lunan
Lentrathan
Ethie
Blairgowrie
FORFAR
Glamis
Monikie
Arbroath or
Aberbrothick
Cupar
Angus
Monyfeith
Strelitz
Dundee
Kinnoul
Errol
FIRTH OF TAY
New-port
Newburgh
St. ANDREWS
Abernethy
CUPAR
Kings Barns
Fife Ness
Crail
May I.
Leven
Anstruther
Largo
KINROSS
L. Leven
FIRTH OF FORTH
Beath
Kirkcaldy
Bass Rock
N. Berwick
Kinghorn
Dunbar
Granton
Inchkeith
Leith
HADDINGTON
St. Abbs Hd.
EDINBURGH
Gifford
Dalkeith
Press
Eyemouth
Lammermuir Hills
Byrecleagh
Ayton
Middleton
BERWICK
Pentland
Muirfoot
Dunse
Tweedmouth
Linton
Lauder
Swinton
Greenlaw
Holy I.
Eddleston
Stow
Blainslie
Coldstream
PEEBLES
R. Tweed
Galashiels
Melrose
KELSO
Biggart

SSTUART.
ESSMAKER
TAIRS UP

CHAPTER FOUR

A Modern City Emerges

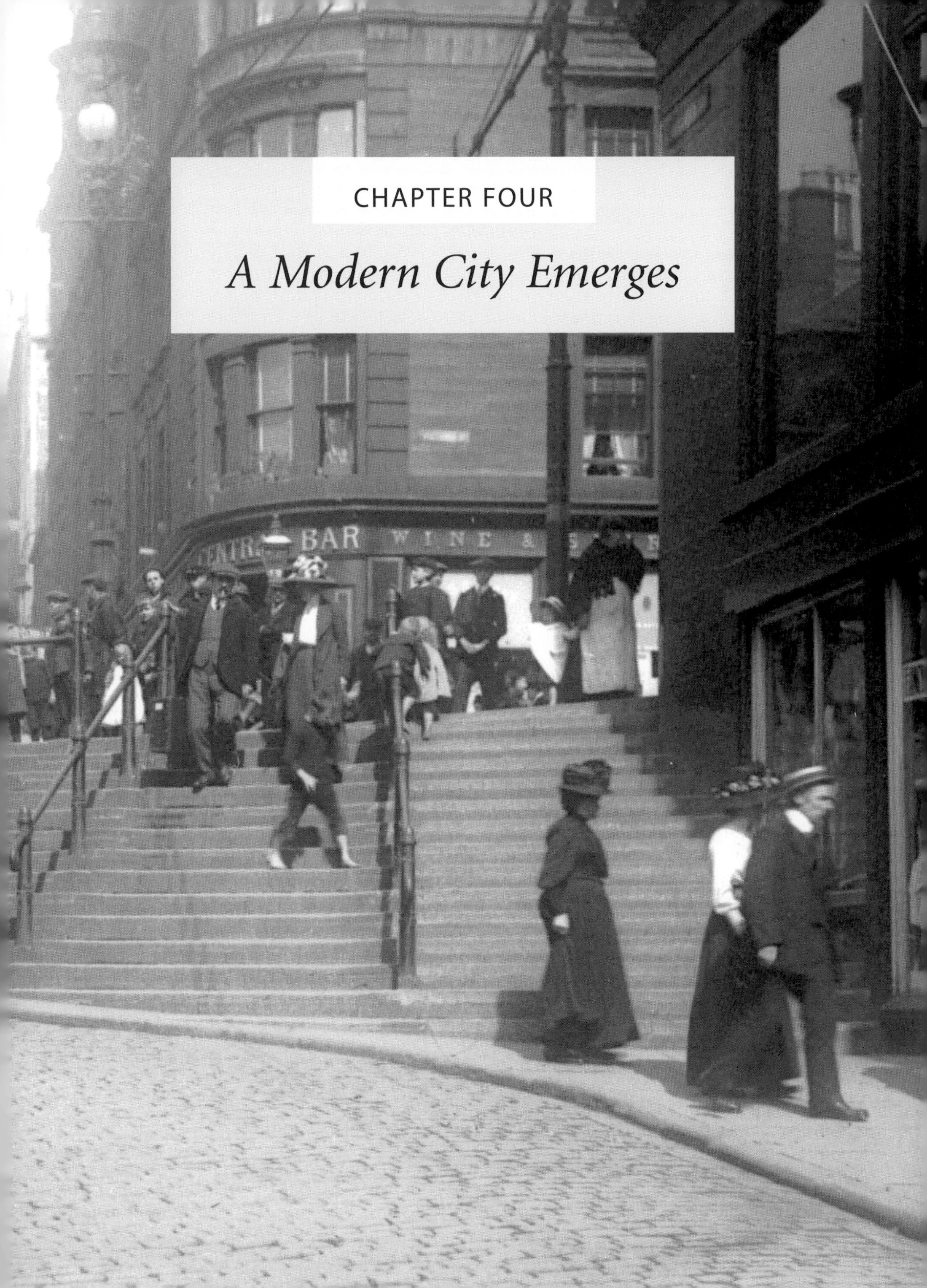

BY THE END of the Victorian era, Dundee had been transformed into a truly industrial city; but Dundee's major problem was that its industry had failed to diversify. Dundee still struggled with the familiar problems of overcrowding and poverty, and the improvements and house building that had begun in the previous century had halted. Most of the working class still lived in tenement housing, and a third of the city's population were still without sanitation. In the Hilltown, Overgate and Blackness Road were slums where life was hard. Most families lived below the poverty line, and outbreaks of infectious disease were still frequent.

In 1906 Dundee saw an upturn in the jute trade, which increased again during the First World War, especially in the production of sandbags. However, there were troubled times ahead for the jute industry, and the end of the war would see a downturn in the jute trade heralding a long and slow demise that would be disastrous for Dundee and its people. Jute was now processed in India, the source of the raw product, where labour costs were significantly lower. Many of the products being made from jute could now also be made from new materials. Dundee was almost wholly dependant on the overseas trade of its jute products; it was ironic that when jute products were needed in Britain it was now cheaper to import them from India.

THE OVERGATE c1895 ZZZ04418 (Dundee City Council, Central Library)

Captain Scott and the RRS 'Discovery'

THE RRS 'DISCOVERY' 2005 D81716k (Gillian Ferguson)

Captain Robert Falcon Scott, or 'Scott of the Antarctic', became a national hero when he completed his National Antarctic Expedition of 1901-04. Dundee shipbuilders built his ship, the RRS 'Discovery', especially for the expedition; through their experience of building whaling ships, they were able to provide Scott with a vessel that could withstand the demanding journey. The ship had to be made of wood, as it was the only material flexible enough to stay intact under the huge pressure of pack ice - an iron ship would have been crushed. Another Dundee ship was used for Scott's fateful second expedition to reach the South Pole. The RRS 'Terra Nova', an Arctic whaler, had been built in Dundee in 1884 and had been used as a relief ship during Scott's first expedition. The 'Terra Nova' became the main ship for his ill-fated race to the Pole in 1910.

THE OVERGATE c1895 ZZZ04418 (Dundee City Council, Central Library)

RAPERY & UNDERCLOTHING
HAIRDRESSER
GIRLS HAIR NEATLY CUT.
LONDON DER
CORONATION FISH SU
STORRIER'S
144

Although little could be done to change the economic difficulties of Dundee at this time, the city was early, in relation to the rest of Britain, in forming plans to combat its social problems. This was mainly thanks to one man, James Thomson, the city engineer and architect. Thomson, who was influenced by Patrick Geddes, started to form an ambitious town plan that would sweep away the last remnants of the medieval town, widen many of the congested arterial routes of the city, and allow Dundee to expand away from the city centre. Thomson's plans were completed in 1910. He proposed a large civic centre at Earl Grey Docks, large-scale slum clearance, plans for a garden suburb, the creation of new housing (which would be rented from the council), suburban road building, and a new city ring road (the Kingsway). Many of Thomson's plans did not come to pass (in part because they were so ambitious, and because of the ensuing war), but many were implemented over time. Even now, Dundonians feel that the shelving of his plans for Dundee's waterfront was a missed opportunity.

Many of Thomson's buildings are still prominent features of the modern cityscape today. The most familiar is the Caird Hall, although by the time this had actually been

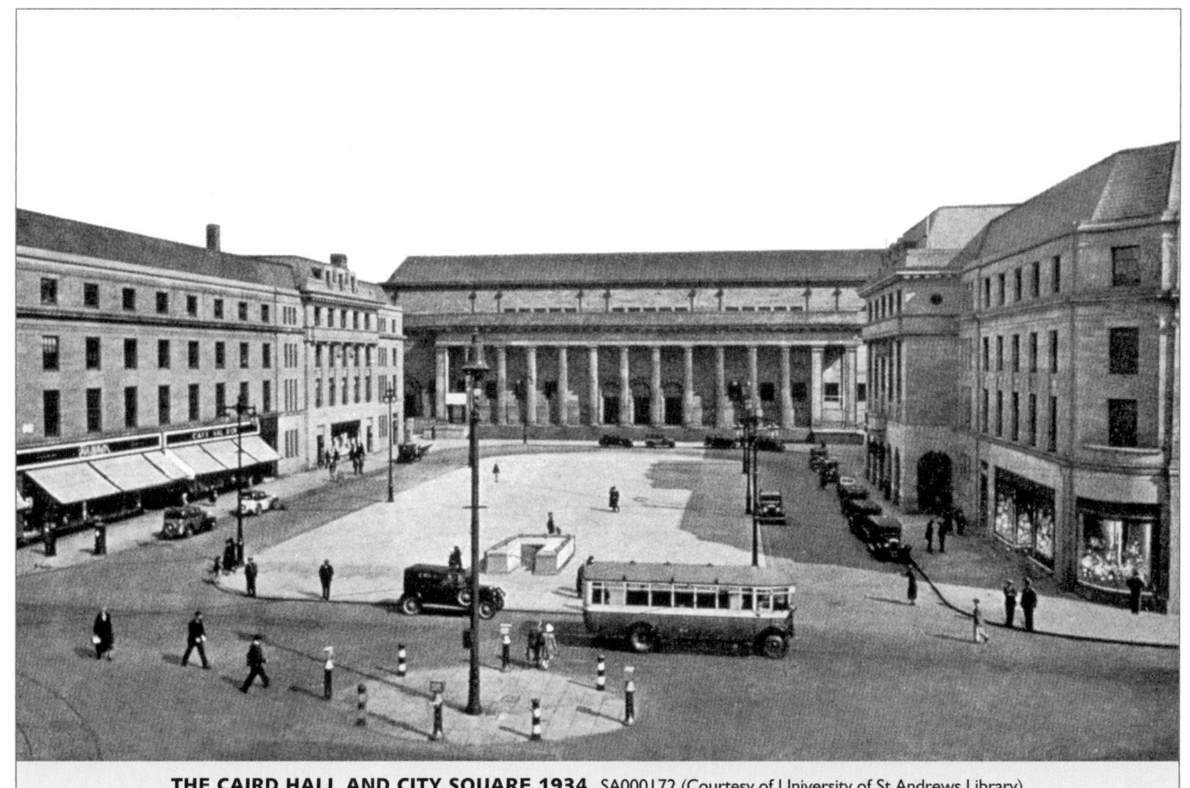

THE CAIRD HALL AND CITY SQUARE 1934 SA000172 (Courtesy of University of St Andrews Library)

built in the 1930s his plans were much modified. Some of Dundee's branch libraries were designed by Thomson, including St Roque's Library in Blackscroft just outside of the city centre, and Barrack Street Museum (originally Ward Road Library). Thomson also pioneered the first municipal housing scheme in Scotland, built just after the First World War; this was in Logie, located beside Balgay Hill. The Craigiebank garden suburb was started by Dundee Corporation and private builders in 1923, and followed Thomson's circular design with small blocks of flats built to look like villas.

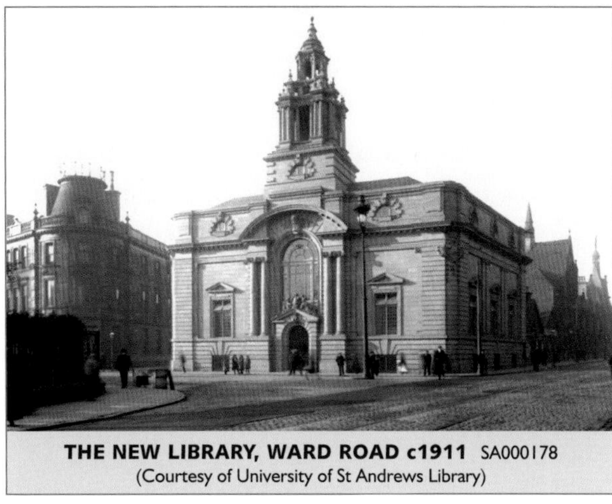

THE NEW LIBRARY, WARD ROAD c1911 SA000178
(Courtesy of University of St Andrews Library)

Now the Barrack Street Museum, this was originally the Ward Road Library. The edge of the Howff is on the left-hand side.

Churchill and the Suffragettes

In 1908 a young Winston Churchill campaigned to become MP for Dundee. Never a supporter of the suffragette movement, Churchill had already had a speech in Manchester interrupted by the campaigners. With such a high number of women workers there, the Votes for Women campaign found strong support from the women of Dundee. The Women's Social and Political Union, led by Emmeline Pankhurst, staged several demonstrations in Dundee, especially when Churchill was in town! Churchill won his campaign, but later suffered a humiliating defeat in 1922; he vowed never to set foot in Dundee again, a vow he kept.

THE COURIER, SATURDAY, MAY 9, 1908.

ANOTHER MANCHESTER?

DEAR WINSTON (thinking)—"Looks a bit fresh—not so safe a seat as I expected. I doubt that reversed saddle is to worry him."

CHURCHILL AND THE SUFFRAGETTES CARTOON 1908
ZZZ04419 (Dundee City Council, Central Library)

At the outbreak of the First World War in 1914 many of Dundee's men enlisted, and Dundee lost a number of its sons in the trenches. Among the horrors of the First World War, Dundee's 4th Battalion of the Black Watch tragically lost over half of their number - over 250 men were killed in the Battle of Loos alone. At home, the Royal Naval Air Service established a seaplane base in Dundee. The F-type hangar, for reconnaissance and submarine operations, had a metal frame with asbestos walls and roof, and was eventually demolished in 1983. After the war a memorial was erected on top of the Law, a constant visual reminder of the sacrifice Dundee had made.

Many of the soldiers who returned to Dundee after the war found the city little changed and prospects bleak. In the 1920s many firms dropped to working a three-day week, and losses were made by even the biggest companies. Some of the companies could not survive; where Dundee had 50 companies involved in jute manufacturing in the 1920s, by 1939 only 32 survived. By the 1930s, employment in the jute industry dropped from 35,000 to 26,000 and continued to decline. At times unemployment in Dundee was twice the national average. The companies that survived made efforts to improve efficiency: wages were lowered, better machinery was introduced, and at times workers were asked to operate two machines.

Unlike jute, some of the smaller industries and businesses within Dundee saw an upturn in profits between the wars. With the creation of Dundee's first industrial estate near the Kingsway, Valentines, publishers of postcards and greeting cards, built a new factory there. They were joined by James Keillor & Sons and Smedley's, who canned raspberries at their new factory. D C Thomson & Co were also doing well, especially with the launch of their comics the Dandy in 1937 and the Beano in 1938. The other two Js, jam and journalism, had joined jute! In 1926, D C Thomson's moved to the red sandstone building in Meadowside that overlooks McManus Galleries. The retail industry also boomed in Dundee: Draffens extended their department store on the Nethergate in 1929, McGill Brothers also extended their store, and so did Alexander Caird & Son in Reform Street.

THE WAR MEMORIAL ON THE LAW 2005 D81717k
(Gillian Ferguson)

Keillor's

The Keillor family business began when a Mrs Keillor invented a new recipe for marmalade after receiving a batch of particularly bitter oranges. Her son, James, established the business, and the company began to produce jam as well as marmalade. The countryside around Dundee has long been famous for growing soft fruit of all kinds – there is even a fruit called a tayberry. In the 1930s James Keillor & Sons moved from their premises in Albert Square to a factory in Dundee's first industrial estate near the Kingsway.

After the First World War new housing was a priority in many of Britain's cities, and certainly much needed in Dundee. Government assistance meant that Dundee Corporation was able to build 8,000 new homes, and the private sector added another 3,000. New residential estates were located near the Kingsway, away from the city centre; some of the earliest were Beechwood and Mid Craigie, created in 1934. It must have been with relief that many of Dundee's citizens left their cramped tenements. For some, council housing remained outwith their reach as it was too expensive, and pockets of slums, like the notorious Overgate, remained in Dundee until as late as the 1960s. Like many places experimenting with the new concept of social housing, Dundee found that its schemes were not without problems. Planned shopping units were often never built, and residents were stranded far from retail and recreational facilities, often with limited public transport links. Where public transport did exist, there were complaints that it was too expensive to get to work or school.

D C Thomson

D C Thomson's publishing company was established in 1905, after an amalgamation of two much older papers, and is still in business today. Among its many publications are The Dundee Courier and The Evening Telegraph (locally known as the 'tele'), and also the more internationally famous Beano, Dandy, Sunday Post and People's Friend. The Courier building, which is still used by the company, can be found on Meadowside across from the McManus Galleries and the High School of Dundee. Legend has it that the Bash Street Kids from the Beano were inspired by the artist Leo Baxendale's view of the children in the playground of the adjacent High School.

DESPERATE DAN 2005
D81718k (Gillian Ferguson)

WEST PARK ROAD 1935 SA000162 (Courtesy of University of St Andrews Library)

West Park Road is an example of the private house building boom in Dundee; it is still a pleasant suburb with views across the Tay.

The run-up to the Second World War again saw an increased demand for sandbags, which helped create jobs in the jute industry. Ship builders in Dundee were also busy building and repairing vessels, especially the Caledon Yard, where a fleet of 'Empire' cargo vessels and HMS 'Activity', an aircraft carrier launched in 1943, were built. The harbour became an important submarine base with French, Dutch, Norwegian and Russian vessels docking there. HMS 'Unicorn' was converted into the headquarters of the naval officer in charge, and visiting Allied solders were billeted in Carolina House Orphanage. Dundee's location meant that it received less war work than the average; instead, Dundee workers were drafted to work in English factories. The 1,300 who were drafted for this purpose were mostly young single women, and only a small number were willing volunteers. Within Dundee, women naturally embraced traditionally male jobs; they laboured on building sites, entered skilled professions like welding, and became conductors on buses and trams.

Dundee was slow to prepare for the coming war, and for a long time did not have enough air raid shelters. When the city did begin to prepare, Court House Square became a depot for storing shelter materials and sandbags. Pavements, lampposts and trees were painted with white stripes to help with visibility during blackouts, and night time driving up the Law was banned. Plans were set in motion to evacuate over 20,000 of Dundee's women, children and infirm into the surrounding Angus countryside. However, only 10,000 people turned up to be evacuated; of those who went, many had soon had enough of country life and returned to the city.

Dundee was relatively unscathed during the war in that only 40 bombs fell on the city, even though Dundee's position on the Tay and the rail bridge might have made it an easy target. The worst air raids took place on 4 and 5 November 1940. On 4 November bombs fell on Dundee, one hitting Baxter Park and bursting a water main. On the night of 5 November a house in Briarwood Terrace was destroyed and a woman killed; a tenement at 19 Rosefield Street suffered a direct hit, although no life was lost. There were also reports of the Forest Park Place electricity sub-station being hit – this was very close to the Forest Park Cinema, where an audience of 250 were watching a film. Not everyone in Dundee heeded the air raid sirens!

At the employment office in Gellatly Street, over 20,000 of Dundee's men joined up to fight for their country. By the end of the war Dundee's war dead numbered 1899. Those left behind in Dundee were particularly generous in their efforts to help the troops when monetary collections were undertaken. A Prisoner of War Appeal Fund Depot was set up in Yeoman Shore, and 142 parcels were handed in from Dundonians to be sent to Germany. When the war finally ended, VE day was celebrated in the city square in May 1945, and so was VJ day, when 50,000 people attended celebrations that went on into the night. The square was floodlit, a welcome change from the blackouts.

After the war, Dundee still suffered from a shortage of housing, and the council built 3,000 pre-fabricated houses, first in Seabraes, then in Douglas, Camperdown and Mains of Fintry. Unlike other towns and cities that were using prefabs as a temporary solution to houses lost through bomb damage, Dundee's prefabs were used to re-house citizens who were still living in poor accommodation. The prefabs were especially popular in Dundee; although the houses were small, many Dundonians loved their prefabs after the constraints of tenement living. Life in the tenements meant little outdoor space of your own, and the prefabs' small gardens and out of town locations must have seemed a rural idyll. Some of the prefabs are still in use in the Ardler area, a testament to the quality of design and materials used for what were intended to be temporary structures. In 1945 the first tenants moved into the Kirkton housing scheme, and five years later 1,500 people were living in the area.

A new air of confidence existed in Dundee after the war. There had been an upturn in the jute market, and the city had been able to attract new industries, especially companies from America. National Cash Registers (popularly known as 'the Cash'), Veeder Root and Timex were all attracted to industrial sites along the Kingsway in the late 1940s and early 1950s. Many manufacturers invested in new machinery, and jute was now important as a backing for carpets, a major growth industry. However, the jute manufacturers were struggling to find workers, and immigrants from Poland, the Ukraine, Italy and Pakistan moved to the city. Schemes for more housing estates were laid down for the Douglas, Fintry, Menzieshill, Ardler and Whitfield areas. New schools were needed, and in 1960 Kirkton High was opened – it was the largest to be built in Scotland since the war. Between 1945 and 1965, 37 new schools were built in Dundee. Private house building was also begun in the 1950s, and bungalows were particularly popular.

In 1946 Princess Elizabeth made her first public appearance in Scotland in Dundee, opening Camperdown Park. By the time of her coronation on 2 June 1953, which was watched by crowds of Dundonians on television screens set up in the Caird Hall, Dundee was thriving. More industries were settling in the city, attracted by the good transport links and industrial estates. Astral, later to become Morphy Richards, was doing well enough in Dundee to move to a new 24-acre site at Gourdie, where they employed 1,200 workers. Bonar Long had become a large export business; they now started to manufacture electrical transformer equipment for power stations. Shipbuilding was still strong in Dundee at the Caledon shipyard, who were now making large oil tankers like the 13,500-ton 'Aida'. The take-up of higher education had also risen, and Duncan of Jordanstone College of Art was opened in the 1950s, reflecting Dundee's long connection with the arts. Dundee's first tower block was also completed in 1958 for the university: this was the Tower Building at the foot of the Perth Road. Following this the university's campus expanded to include a new student union, a dental school and new student residences.

Did you know?

Famous names at the Caird Hall

In the 1950s Dundee played host to a number of famous performers such as Bob Hope, Danny Kaye, Mario Lanza and Frank Sinatra (only 600 tickets were sold for his first night), whilst in the 1960s both the Beatles and the Rolling Stones played at the Caird Hall.

Dundee's Football Clubs

Dundee, despite its size, has two high-profile football teams: Dundee Football Club, founded in 1893 and located at Dens Park since 1919, and located across the road at Tannadice Park, Dundee United Football Club, dating from 1909. The Dundee Derby, when the two rivals play one another, is one of the most anticipated matches for the fans of both teams.

During the 1950s, coffee bars became popular with the young; the Coffee Cup was opened in Albert Street, and 40s in Dura Street. Although dance halls such as the Palais, the Locarno, and the West End Palais had been all the rage during the Second World War, in the 1950s their popularity decreased, although the Empress Ballroom at Victoria Dock was still well used by the older generation. Jazz was now fashionable with the opening of the Dundee Jazz Club in Parker Street and in 1961 the Tomb in Nicoll Street.

The cinema was always a favourite pastime of Dundonians. During the 1930s Dundee boasted 31 cinemas, more per head than anywhere else in Scotland. In 1936, when Green's Playhouse Cinema first opened, it was celebrated as the second largest cinema in Europe, with seating for over 4,000. During the Second World War the Caird Hall was also converted into a cinema to meet Dundee's demand for 'the pictures'!

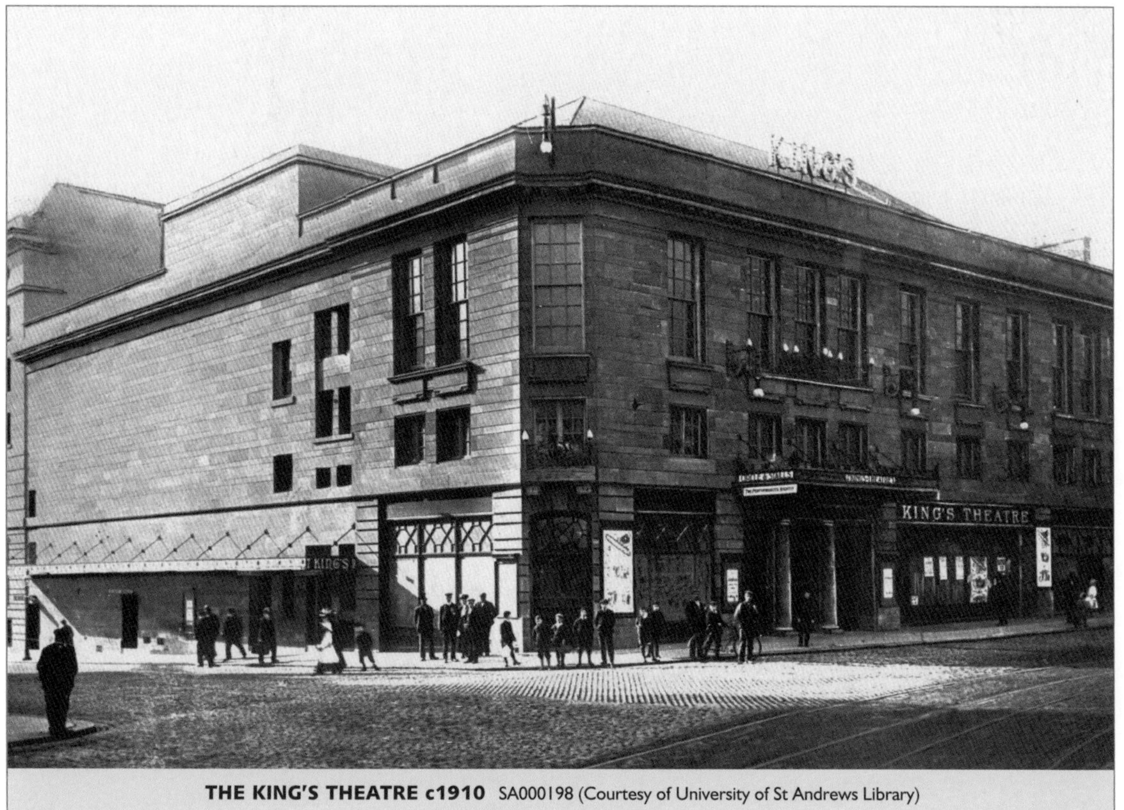

THE KING'S THEATRE c1910 SA000198 (Courtesy of University of St Andrews Library)

Built in 1909, the King's Theatre was the most outstanding of Dundee's theatres. The auditorium was opulently decorated with gilded plaster mouldings and dark crimson upholstery. There was also a superb domed ceiling with frescoes. Marie Lloyd and Harry Lauder were just two of the famous names to play the King's. Today the King's still exists as a nightclub.

WEST PARK ROAD c1930 SA000162 (Courtesy of University of St Andrews Library)

Did you know?

Mills Observatory, located at the top of Balgay Hill, is the only full-time public observatory still in use. It is hard to believe, but the dome was originally made of papier mache.

MILLS OBSERVATORY SA000166
(Courtesy of University of St Andrews Library)

By the 1980s only three cinemas remained in Dundee, and the Dundee Rep theatre company was homeless. The company was established in 1939 and had used Foresters Hall, off Ward Road, as their premises until they were destroyed by fire. After a long period of fundraising, new premises were built in South Tay Street in 1982. Some of the famous names who first trod the boards with the company include Glenda Jackson, Michael York and Brian Cox, and the company is very much involved in community theatre.

During the 1960s the rise of motorised transport for both goods and passengers caused Dundee East station to close in 1960, and then Dundee West in 1965 - all trains now used the Tay Bridge station. Steam trains had been replaced by diesel engines. A new bus station was also built in 1958 at the bottom of the Seagate. By 1960 the 'Fifie' was ferrying much more vehicular traffic across the Tay, and on 18 August 1966 the new Tay Road Bridge was opened by the Queen Mother, much improving Dundee's road transport links. The first weekend the bridge opened, over 60,000 people drove across it and experienced what is still today one of the best ways to view the city.

DUNDEE REP THEATRE 2005 D81719k (Gillian Ferguson)

However, the building of the bridge had brought major changes and the demolition of the dock area. Added to this were plans to improve the city centre with the clearance of the old Overgate, Wellgate, Hawkhill and Hilltown areas; these were to be replaced by modern shopping malls and high-rise housing. Even at the time it was felt by some that the heart had been ripped from Dundee with the loss of so many historical buildings. The demolishing of the Royal Arch is still lamented in Dundee today. There were appeals for a reversal of the demolition of Dundee West Station, but to no avail. The city was committed to modernisation, even though many thought that the new concrete buildings were ugly.

THE ROYAL ARCH 1878 SA000121 (Courtesy of University of St Andrews Library)

The original arch, built in 1844 to commemorate a visit from Queen Victoria, was constructed from wood. This was replaced by a sandstone arch in 1850. The Royal Arch was demolished to make way for the Tay Road Bridge.

CALEDONIAN RAILWAY STATION c1890 SA000168 (Courtesy of University of St Andrews Library)

Caledonian Railway Station or Dundee West Station, situated at the bottom of Union Street, was built in 1870 and demolished in the 1960s.

By the early 1970s the new Overgate complex was completed; it boasted two shopping levels, an office block, a police station and public lavatories. One of the problems with the complex was that after the shops closed it became deserted. The 'old' Overgate is wistfully described by some as comparable to York's Shambles, and although this may be an exaggeration, it had been a colourful mix of shops and houses; although it was dilapidated, there was a strong sense of community in the area. The pouring of concrete into the centre of Dundee continued with the building of the council offices of Tayside House, still visible above the Caird Hall.

A new leisure centre was built on the waterfront in 1974 with an Olympic-sized pool, a smaller training pool, a children's pool and a diving pool. The Olympia leisure centre and Tay Bridge railway station were now cut off from the city centre by a network of roads and dual carriageways. Pedestrian walkways high above these roads (rather than underground underpasses) were built as the solution to reaching the waterfront developments. Lochee High Street was also transformed in the 1970s with the building of a small indoor shopping centre and linked supermarket. Unlike the Overgate, this was more successful in Lochee; the reason was that the complex included some housing, and many of the traditional shops survived to give a pleasing mix of the old and the new.

Another Dundee landmark that was to disappear in the 1970s was the Wellgate steps, replaced in 1977 by the Wellgate Centre. The Wellgate was another area with a mixture of tenement flats and small shops, situated along the route from the Murraygate to the Hilltown. The new Wellgate Shopping Centre was a modern mall built on three levels; as well as major chain stores in large units, it included a market hall with small shops and stalls. The Wellgate Shopping Centre also included a small cinema, and today is still the home of Dundee Central Libraries. This new mall was to be much more successful than the Overgate complex, and a downturn of the Overgate's fortunes began.

Did you know?

General Monck's House at the entrance of the Overgate with its unusual circular corner tower was for centuries an early tourist attraction in Dundee. It survived until the 1960s, when it was demolished to make way for the new shopping centre.

MONCK'S HOUSE c1895 ZZZ04420 (Dundee City Council, Central Library)

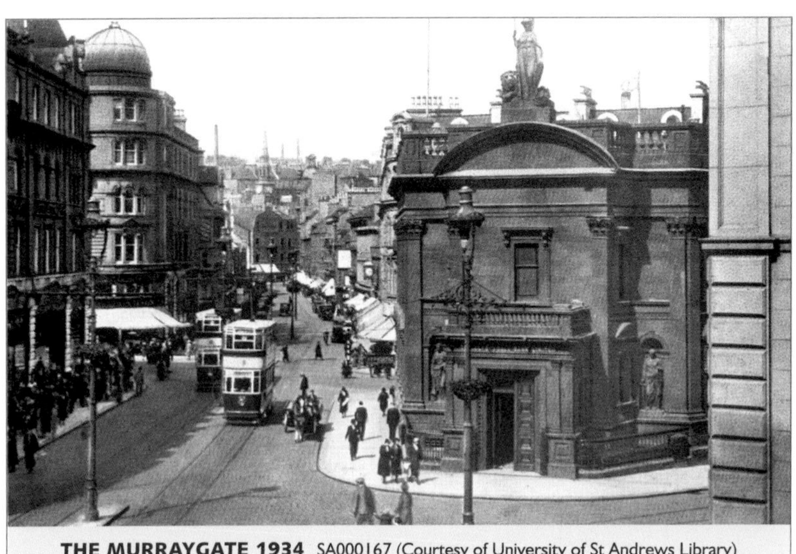

THE MURRAYGATE 1934 SA000167 (Courtesy of University of St Andrews Library)

Today this view of the Murraygate remains much the same. The area has been pedestrianised, and a feature has been made of the tram tracks. At the far end of the Murraygate the old Wellgate is still visible.

By the end of the 1970s Dundee had begun to experience an economic downturn and a rise in unemployment that would continue well into the 1980s. By 1977 only 14 of the jute firms were still in operation, and the other industries that had flourished in the city started to struggle. NCR's workforce fell from its peak of 6,500 to less than 1,000. The Caledon shipyard could not compete with firms in the Far East, and it eventually closed in 1982. The service sector was now a bigger employer than the industrial sector, and accounted for two thirds of the city's workforce. Ninewells Hospital opened on the western edge of the city in 1974 with 31 wards, over 700 beds, 3,200 staff and car parking for 900 cars. Dundee Royal Infirmary was still in use, and was improved in the 1970s.

The Dundee Project, begun in the 1980s, had a budget of £24,000,000 for the implementation of improvement projects across Dundee, and in 1980 the Blackness area was designated Scotland's first industrial improvement area. Improvements in Blackness included a series of public art works, many relating to the city's past, but unfortunately the project did not have long-term success. Investors were offered tax incentives and custom-built serviced sites if they located in Dundee and in the new Technology Park located at the west end of the city. On a more ambitious scale, and more successful than the Blackness scheme, the Technology Park attracted General Accident to re-locate their service centre from London to Dundee. Many of the units sat unused in the Technology Park for some time until the arrival of several call centres, which employed around 2,000 Dundonians.

By the late 1980s, however, the city that had witnessed much change and lost much of its confidence was developing a new identity and beginning to revive again. Captain Scott's RRS 'Discovery' returned to the city in 1986; after major refurbishment it became a symbol for Dundee, which would now be known as 'The City of Discovery'. By 1993, the excellent Discovery Quay was completed as an interpretation centre and permanent home for the 'Discovery'; the ship was opened to the public, and is now a major tourist attraction.

In 1991 Dundee celebrated its 800th birthday, with festivities throughout the year. The most memorable was a day-long street carnival in the city centre when delegates from Dundee's twin cities, Orléans, Alexandria, Wurzburg and Zadar saw bands playing, re-enactments of scenes from the city's history, and a fly-over by RAF jets. Many will also remember the gasometer in East Dock Street decorated like a giant birthday cake for that year.

Did you know?

Dundee on Film

Dundee has featured in a number of films over the years. In 1983 the Caird Hall stood in for the Bolshoi Theatre in 'An Englishman Abroad'. In 1988 the High School played the part of the Berlin Reichstag and the then dilapidated Camperdown Works the role of bombed Berlin in 'Christabel', scripted by Dennis Potter. More recently, Dundee played itself in the BBC's 'Jute City', a detective story set in the city.

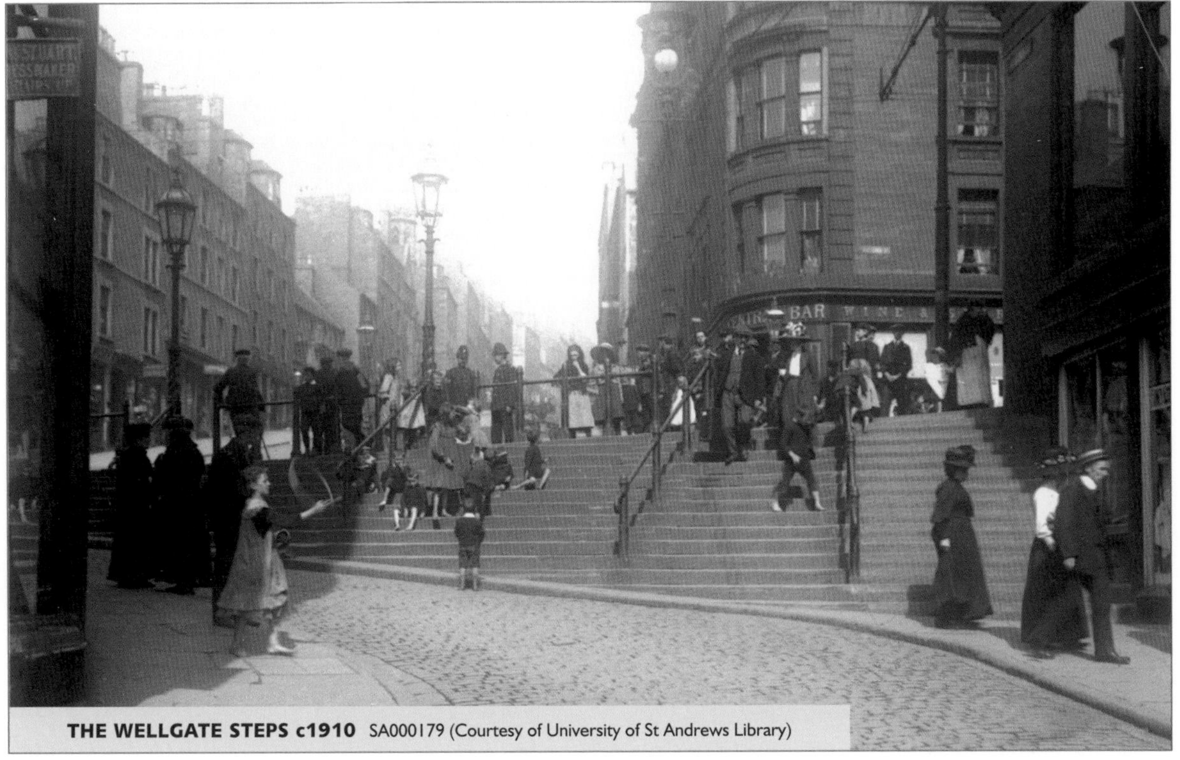

THE WELLGATE STEPS c1910 SA000179 (Courtesy of University of St Andrews Library)

This view from the foot of the Wellgate steps looks up the Hilltown. Even at this late date many of the children are still without shoes.

CHAPTER FIVE

Dundee Rediscovered

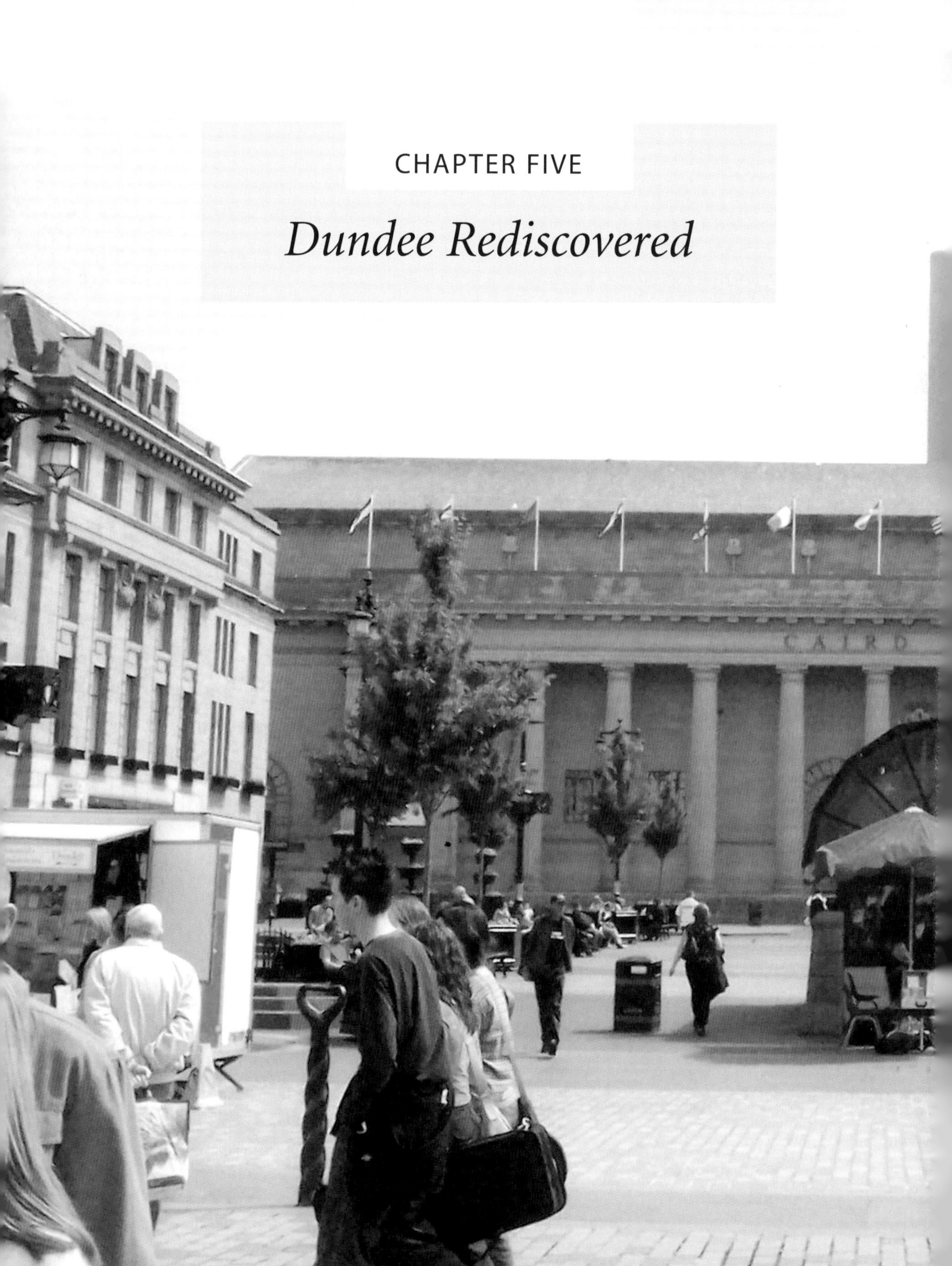

Caird Hall

DUNDEE TODAY is an exciting place to live in or visit, with the city experiencing a new optimism and confidence. At last the city has begun to appreciate its historical assets, to encourage new high-quality developments and to build on its unique attributes. The city's identity is still strong. It is a vibrant, bustling and modern place, which recognises and respects its past. Although Dundee has been battered and bruised throughout its history, its resilience has always shone through; today Dundee is again reaping the rewards of its unique situation and identity. The self-confidence of the city has grown, and it is finally making the most of its position on one of the most beautiful waterways in Europe. Dundonians are renowned for their friendliness and self-deprecating humour, and have always had an enduring love for the city of their birth. During the mass-modernising of the city in the 1960s and 70s, many Dundonians lamented the death and loss of the old parts of the city, partly for its loss of character, but mainly for the loss of Dundee's community spirit.

In the last few years of the 20th century, Dundee was the focus of a number of projects that reflected Dundee's new confidence and character. Verdant Works, opened in 1997, embraces and celebrates Dundee's industrial past and the workforce whose labour helped to build the city. The museum is housed in a former jute works, and incorporates much of the machinery used in the

Gardyne's Land

Hidden behind later buildings on the High Street, and accessed through the atmospheric Gray's Close, Gardyne's Land is the oldest residential building to survive in Dundee. The house was built for a prosperous merchant, and its sophistication is an indicator of Dundee's early wealth and status. Much altered over time, and with little of its original interior surviving, Gardyne's Land and the adjoining buildings on the High Street are currently being restored by the excellent Tayside Building Preservation Trust with plans to create a five-star backpackers' hostel, much needed in Dundee.

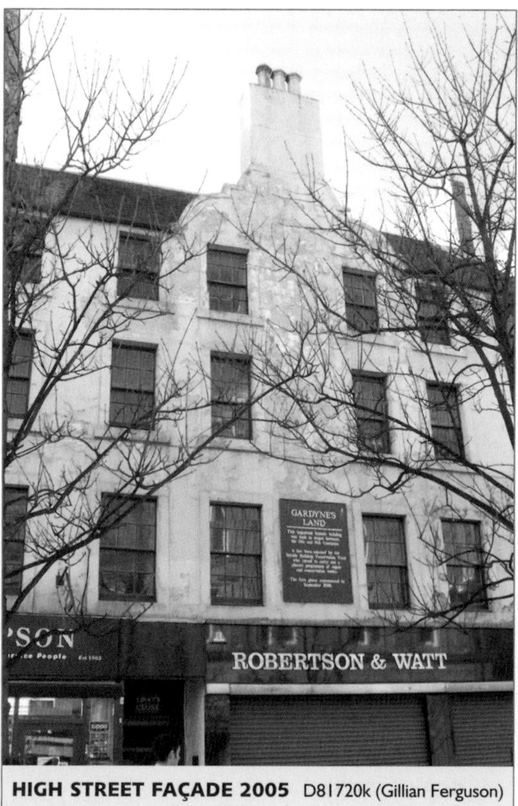

HIGH STREET FAÇADE 2005 D81720k (Gillian Ferguson)

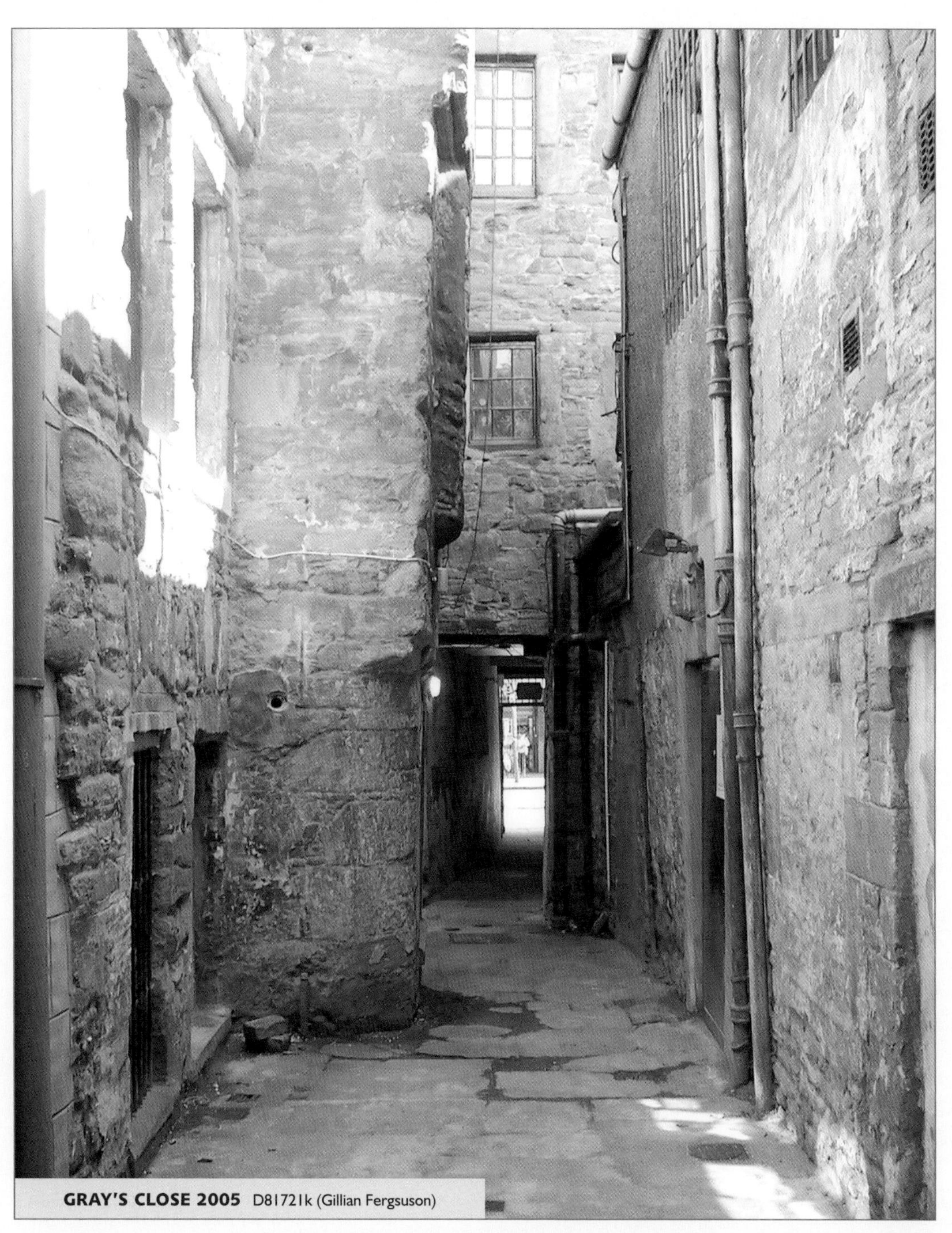

GRAY'S CLOSE 2005 D81721k (Gillian Fergsuson)

processing of jute. The museum also tells the personal stories of the workers and the owners, and creates an evocative memory of mill life. Another popular attraction, Sensation, is an innovative science centre based on the five senses. Built at a cost of £5,000,000, the centre opened in July 2000 and has over 60 interactive exhibits.

The creation of the Dundee Contemporary Arts Centre (DCA) in 1999 put Dundee at the cutting edge of modern art, and helped to develop the idea of a 'cultural quarter' in the city. The cultural quarter at the foot of the Perth Road and along the Westport has at its heart Dundee University's campus, and includes the Dundee Rep theatre and many high-quality individual retailers. The cultural quarter's many bars and restaurants come alive at night, and are an exciting place to spend an evening. More culture can be found at the McManus Galleries, where Dundee's wonderful art collection is displayed and its history celebrated in an excellent museum. The McManus Galleries is currently undergoing a major refurbishment, both internally and externally, that will free it from its road-dominated setting; much of the area will be pedestrianised, and garden spaces and a terraced area created. The museum within Broughty Ferry Castle has also recently been updated, and is well worth a visit. Here much can be learned about Dundee's military past, the whaling industry, and the ecology of the area.

SENSATION 2005 D81727k (Gillian Ferguson)

The DCA

Opened in 1999, the Dundee Contemporary Arts centre (DCA) has attracted over 900,000 visitors since its opening. DCA has been successful in attracting several international artists' work to Dundee, and there is a strong focus on community activities. The centre includes five floors of galleries, a print centre, educational facilities and the University of Dundee visual research centre. Incorporated within the building is the Jute Cafe Bar, a busy restaurant and popular nightspot.

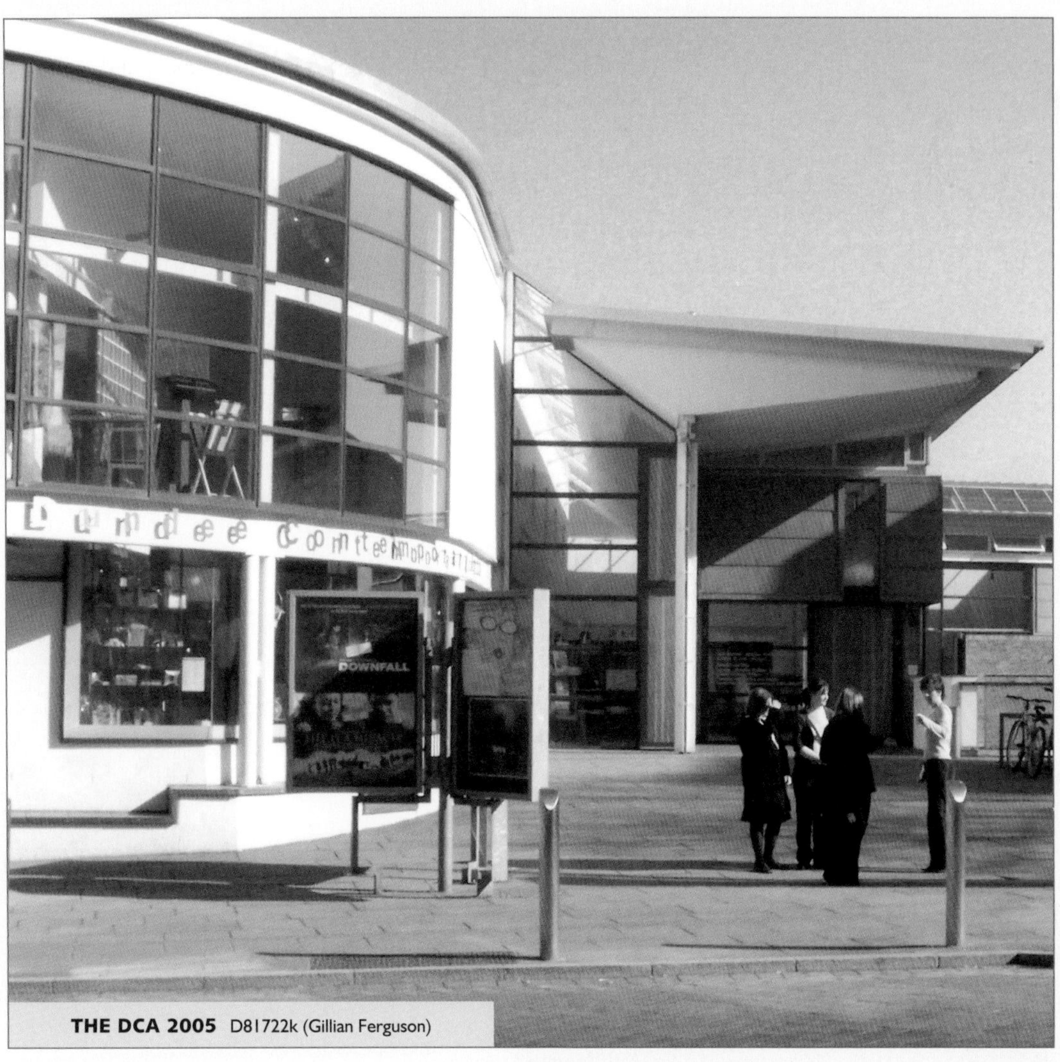

THE DCA 2005 D81722k (Gillian Ferguson)

THE CITY QUAY 2005 D81723k (Gillian Ferguson)

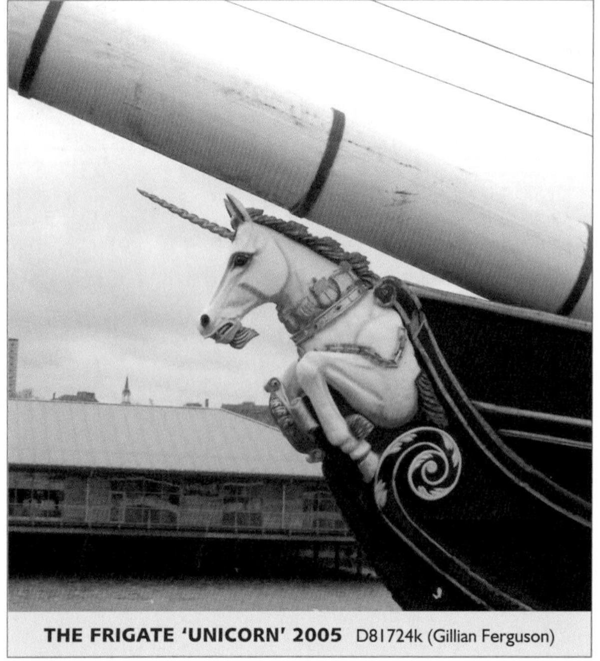

THE FRIGATE 'UNICORN' 2005 D81724k (Gillian Ferguson)

Dundee has begun to find better ways of linking the city centre with its greatest asset, the waterfront. The Victoria Dock, now known as the City Quay, and surviving dockyard sheds have been converted into retail units and restaurants, with the addition of the New Apex Hotel and a luxury flat and townhouse development. The Victoria Dock is also home to two treasures of Dundee's maritime heritage, the frigate 'Unicorn' and the North Carr lightship. Some of the equipment and fittings within the lightship date from its commission in 1933, and it has recently undergone conservation. The 46-gun 'Unicorn' is the oldest floating warship, dating from 1824, and is gradually undergoing conservation works.

Dundee has recently become a Mecca for shoppers with the redevelopment of the Overgate Centre and the creation of several new retail parks. The Overgate centre is a light, airy and thoroughly modern shopping mall whose glass frontage reflects the City Churches. It has proved to be popular with Dundonians, and its wealth of high street stores has had the effect of drawing shoppers from outwith the city's boundaries. The Kingsway West Retail Park has been extended and has created out-of-town shopping which compliments city centre stores. The Gallagher Retail Park on East Dock Street has made use of the listed Gourlay Works, an iron-framed foundry building dating from 1870 where parts for the 'Discovery' were built. One of Britain's earliest aviation pioneers, Preston Watson, developed his experimental winged flying machine known as the 'wiggle-waggle' at the plant. This ambitious project has seen the building dismantled, rotated 180 degrees and moved several yards to a new position. Much of the stone could not be re-used, but the iron frame has been retained, and some of the stone has been used to create an attractive wall for the park.

CITY SQUARE TODAY 2005 D81725k (Gillian Ferguson)

New leisure facilities have also been created in Dundee, giving locals and visitors plenty to do in their spare time. Bingo is, as ever, popular in the city, and new state-of-the-art halls and improved facilities have continued to attract new generations of players. In 1997 Greens Playhouse was given an £8,500,000 upgrade by Mecca Bingo to become one of the largest bingo halls in the country. Bingo is played in Lochee and Douglas in purpose-built Gala clubs, and buses bring players from smaller towns outwith the city to play in Dundee.

The Olympia Leisure centre has also been refurbished, and the main pool is now a 'fun pool' with three exhilarating water flumes and a wave machine. With the closure of the Kingsway Ice Rink, Dundee was left for many years without ice skating facilities. A new rink has been built at the Camperdown Leisure Park, and Dundee once again has an ice hockey team, the Texol Stars. The ice can also be covered and the space used to stage other large events such as the Dundee Spring Flower Show. Visiting the cinema is still popular in Dundee; the city has two multiplexes, one at the Camperdown Leisure Park and another in the east of the city at Douglasfield. For a more intimate cinema experience, the DCA has two screens, and along with mainstream films specialises in showing independent productions. Film festivals at DCA regularly have an international theme, with French, German and Italian seasons all on offer.

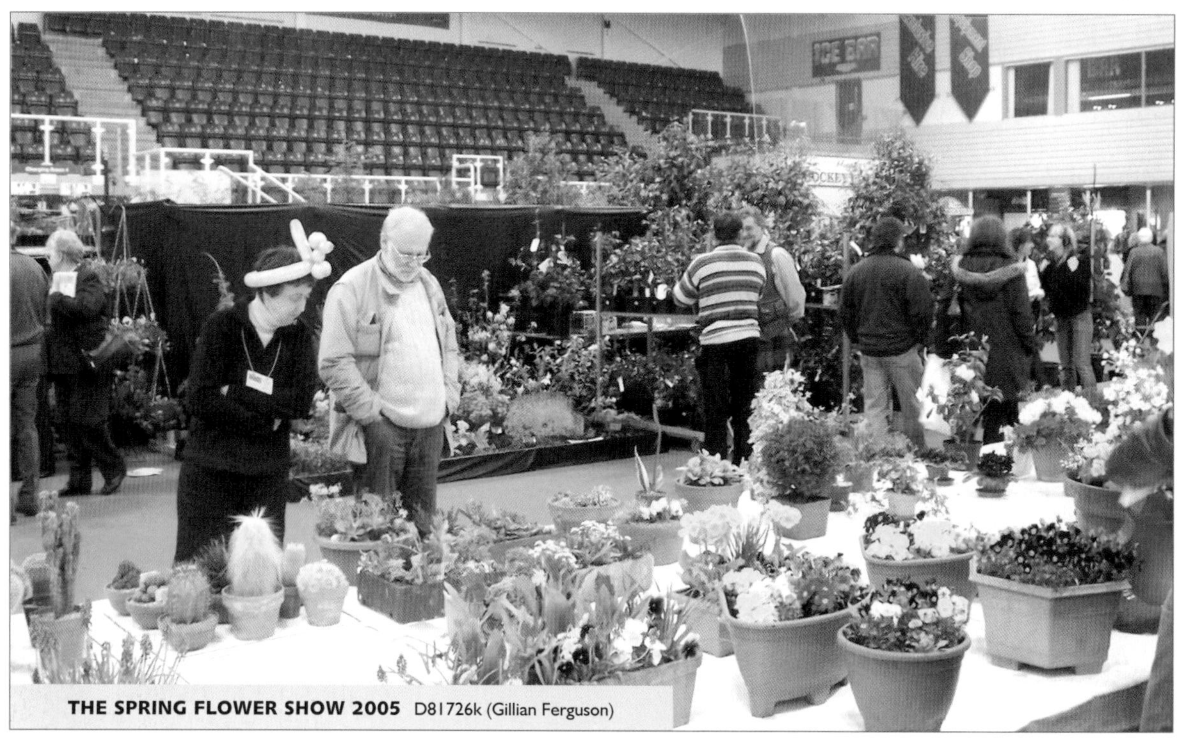

THE SPRING FLOWER SHOW 2005 D81726k (Gillian Ferguson)

Dundee still retains its many green spaces and parks, and they are well used by locals and visitors. Baxter Park has also been returned to its former glory with the reinstatement of its impressive wrought iron gates and railings and a return to the park's original formal layout. Plans are in place to renovate the pavilion into a tearoom and hospitality suite, and an urban ranger's centre on the site of the former bandstand is designed to encourage community activity. Camperdown Park is a popular destination every Easter for Dundee children to roll their eggs, and the park hosts an array of Easter activities. The park also includes a golf course, a zoo, an adventure playground, and rowing boats for hire, and throughout the summer there is a carnival. The popular children's play park at Castle Green in Broughty Ferry has also been recently revamped, and the golden sands of Broughty Ferry beach still see Dundonians flock there from all over the city in hot weather.

Higher educational facilities have gone from strength to strength in recent years in Dundee. The city is now home to the Scottish Contemporary School of Dance, located in their new building The Space on the Kingsway campus of Dundee College. As well as full-time courses, The Space offers a range of part-time and evening dance classes from novice to advanced stages in an array of dance styles including belly dancing and salsa.

THE WELLCOME TRUST BIOCENTRE 2005 D81728k (Gillian Ferguson)

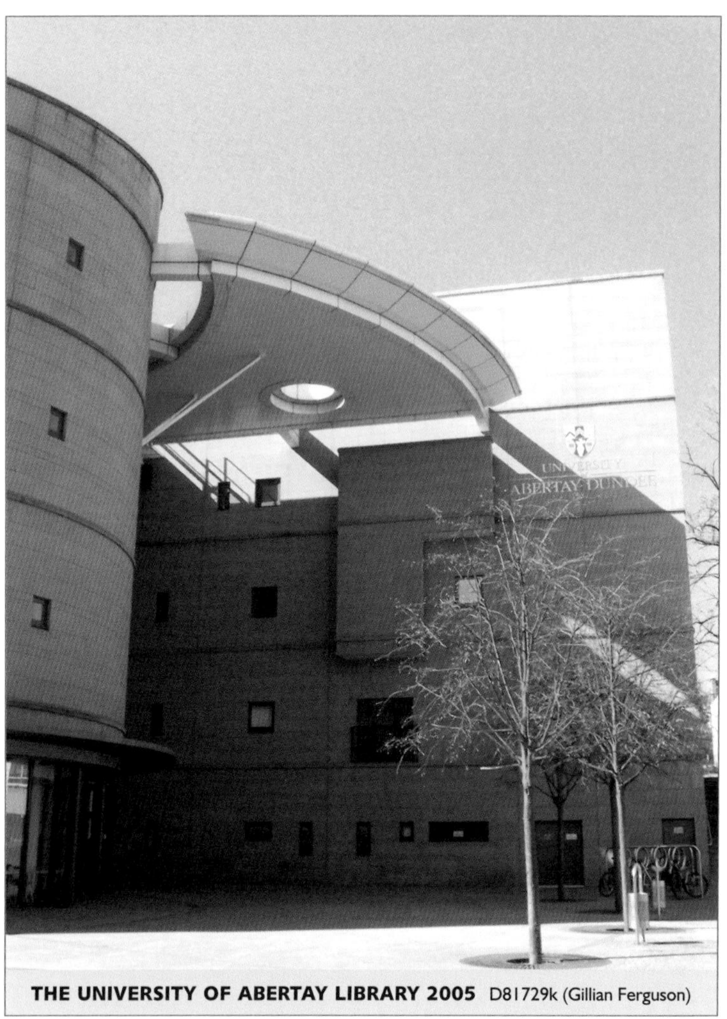

THE UNIVERSITY OF ABERTAY LIBRARY 2005 D81729k (Gillian Ferguson)

Recently Dundee's two universities have also continued to grow. In the last five years, the University of Dundee has doubled in size, and presently has over 12,000 students. The internationally renowned Wellcome Trust Biocentre, part of the university, is one of Dundee's biggest successes. The centre currently has 250 scientists leading research into diabetes, cancer and stem cells. Dundee's newest university, the University of Abertay, has over 5,000 students; its state-of-the-art library facilities in Bell Street were opened by Her Majesty the Queen in 1988. The university, currently ranked as the best in Scotland for environmental research, is also a world leader in computer arts and computer games technology, and is home to the International Centre for Computer Games and Visual Entertainment.

One of Dundee's newest, and most sophisticated, buildings is Maggie's Centre, designed by the internationally famous architect Frank Gehry in 2003. Gehry's friend Maggie Keswick Jencks, who died of cancer in 1995, inspired the centre. The centre provides day-care for cancer patients; it was built in the grounds of Ninewells Hospital after a major charity fundraising campaign. The building commands magnificent views over the Firth of Tay, and is a calming, friendly and invigorating place for patients to spend time.

Did you know?

Dundee was voted the 'Friendliest Campus in Scotland', according to the 'Virgin Guide to British Universities'. The city has the tag 'Scotland's univerCity', and there are more students per head of population here than anywhere else in Scotland.

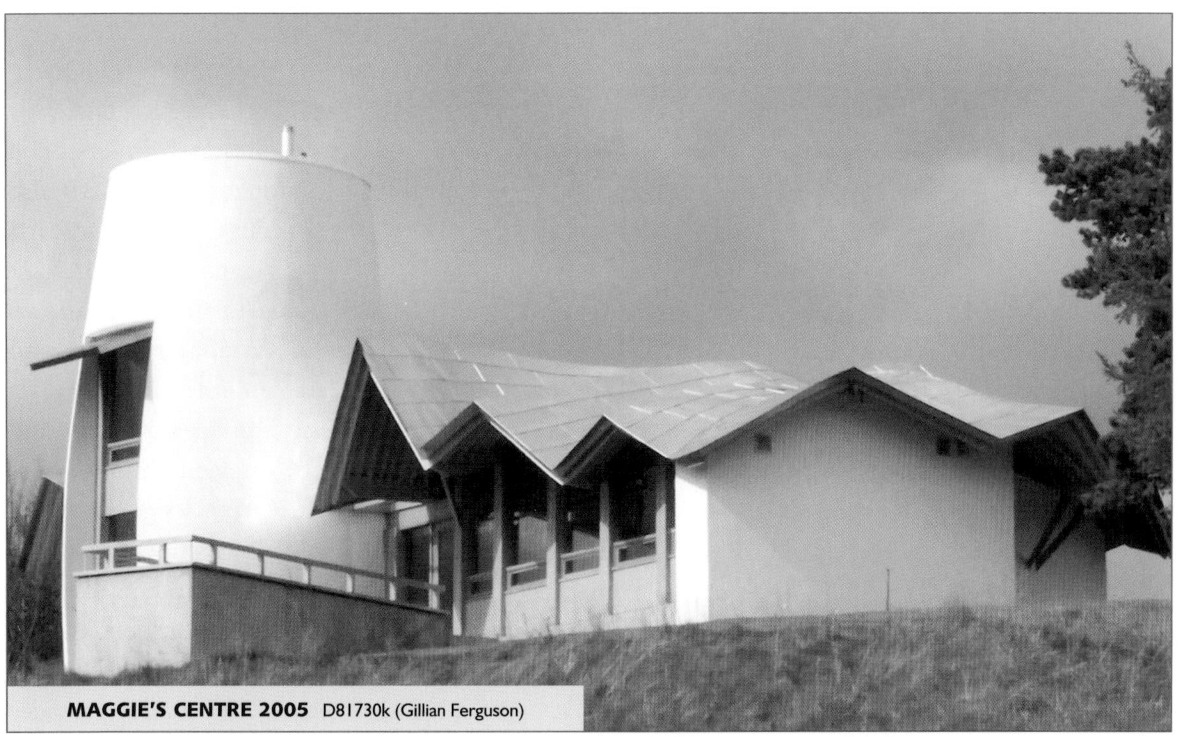

MAGGIE'S CENTRE 2005 D81730k (Gillian Ferguson)

Did you know?

The Dundee Book Prize

The Dundee Book Prize was first established in 2000 and attracted 82 entries. Run in conjunction by the City of Discovery Campaign and the University of Dundee, the £6000 prize also includes the publication of the winning novel. Although novels on any theme and of any genre can be entered, the first two winners both chose to set their novels in the city.

Dundee is also in the process of creating a £20,000,000 Digital Media Park on the site of a former railway goods yard located in the Seabraes. The development, close to the Universities of Dundee and Abertay, will put the city at the forefront of digital media, and will radically redevelop a neglected area of Dundee's city centre.

Dundee is also about to witness one of its most ambitious and dramatic redevelopments in recent history. Over the next 30 years, the waterfront of the city centre will be radically transformed. The area, which is generally regarded as one of the city's unused gems, will be the site of a number of major developments aimed at improving and celebrating the waterfront's unique viewpoint and setting. The area has long been separated from the city centre by the dual carriageway that runs along the waterfront. Over the next few years, however, the redevelopment will extend the city centre down to the water, with greater access for walkers and cyclists. The ramps of the Tay Road Bridge will be moved to create a more open space, and the waterfront will be transformed into a continental-style boulevard, lined with trees. Added to this will be the creation of a new dock and marina, a redevelopment of the railway station, and the formation of a major new civic square. It is ironic that the plans recall the aims of James Thomson, who had similar ideas for the city at the turn of the 19th century.

The city is now home to many exciting and colourful events. During summer weekends, the 'Summer in the City' programme provides a calendar of different activities in the streets of the city centre. The stalls from the visiting farmers' market and the continental market are now a familiar sight in the city centre throughout the year. The Spring Flower Show, bringing a splash of colour to April, has moved to the larger venue of Dundee Ice Arena, and the Flower and Food Festival, held in Camperdown Park, has grown in size and reputation, and now attracts major visitor numbers to Dundee. The city also has a lively music scene: major concerts from classical to rock are held at the Caird Hall, and live music can be heard at a variety of smaller venues throughout the city.

It would seem that the city and its people retain the ability to embrace change and to take chances to find new ways to grow and prosper. One thing is certain: whether you have long known the city, or are a new visitor, there is always something exciting to discover in Dundee.

Did you know?

The Blues Bonanza

The annual blues festival, the Dundee Blues Bonanza, which is held every July, is the biggest in Europe. For three days hundreds of musicians and fans descend on the city to celebrate the music that they love.

ACKNOWLEDGMENTS

Thanks are due to Dundee Central Libraries, Dundee University Library and Archives, and Dundee City Archives. I would like to thank my family and friends for all their help, patience and support, especially Mum and Dad, Billy, Violet and Catherine.

FURTHER READING LIST

W Brown: Early Days in a Dundee Mill 1819-23. Abertay Historical Publications 1980
A J Cook (ed): Baxter's of Dundee. University of Dundee 1980
E Gauldie: Cruel Habitations. George Allen & Unwin Ltd 1974
D A MacMurchie: I remember another Princes Street! Lochee Publications Ltd 1986
C McKean and D Walker: Dundee - An Illustrated Architectural Guide. RIAS Books 1993
L Miskell, C A Whatley and B Harris (eds): Victorian Dundee: Image and Realities. Tuckwell Press 2000
A M Scott: Discovering Dundee. Mercat Press 1999
A M Scott: Modern Dundee: Life in the City Since World War Two. Breedon Books 2002
The Dundee Textile Industry. Scottish Historical Society 1969
Dundee on Record: Images of the Past. RCAHMS Publishing 1992
W Stewart Howe: The Dundee Textile Industry 1960-1977. Aberdeen University Press 1982
E P D Torrie: Medieval Dundee. Abertay Historical Society 1990
D M Walker: Dundee Architecture and Architects 1750-1914. Abertay Historical Publications 1977
M Watson: Jute and Flax Mills in Dundee. Huttun Press Ltd 1990
C A Whatley, D B Swinfen and A M Smith: The Life and Times of Dundee. John Donald Publishers 1993

Photographs used by courtesy of University of St Andrews Library are reproduced from digital copies of the originals held in the University of St Andrews Library. For further information about the collections, obtaining copies of images, or authorisation to reproduce them, please refer to http://specialcollections.st-and.ac.uk or contact Department of Special Collections, University of St Andrews Library, North Street, St Andrews, Fife KY16 9TR (tel 01334-462339); email speccoll@st-and.ac.uk

THE ALEXANDRA FOUNTAIN 1907 D81001t

Ottakar's Bookshops

Ottakar's bookshops, the first of which opened in Brighton in 1988, can now be found in over 130 towns and cities across the United Kingdom. Expansion was gradual throughout the 1990s, but the chain has expanded rapidly in recent years, with many new shop openings and the acquisition of shops from James Thin and Hammicks.

Ottakar's has always known that a shop's local profile is as important, if not more important, than the chain's national profile, and has encouraged its staff to make their shops a part of the local community, tailoring stock to suit the area and forging links with local schools and businesses.

Local history has always been a strong area for Ottakar's, and the company has published its own award winning local history titles, based on text written by its customers, in recent years.

With a reputation for friendly, intelligent and enthusiastic booksellers, warm, inviting shops with an excellent range of books and related products, Ottakar's is now one of the UK's most popular booksellers. In 2003 and then again in 2004 it won the prestigious Best Bookselling Company of the Year Award at the British Book Awards.

Ottakar's has commissioned The Francis Frith Collection to create a series of town history books similar to this volume, as well as a range of stylish gift products, all illustrated with historical photographs.

Participating Ottakar's bookshops can be found in the following towns and cities:

Aberdeen
Abergavenny
Aberystwyth
Andover
Ashford
Ayr
Banbury
Barnstaple
Basildon
Berkhamsted
Bishop's Stortford
Boston
Brentwood
Bromley
Bury St Edmunds
Camberley
Canterbury
Carmarthen
Chatham
Chelmsford
Cheltenham
Cirencester
Coventry
Crawley
Darlington
Dorchester
Douglas, Isle of Man
Dumfries
Dundee
East Grinstead
Eastbourne
Elgin
Enfield
Epsom
Falkirk
Fareham
Farnham
Folkestone
Glasgow
Gloucester
Greenwich
Grimsby
Guildford
Harrogate
Hastings
Haywards Heath
Hemel Hempstead
High Wycombe
Horsham
Huddersfield
Inverness
Isle of Wight
Kendal
King's Lynn
Kirkcaldy
Lancaster
Lincoln
Llandudno
Loughborough
Lowestoft
Luton
Lymington
Maidenhead
Maidstone
Market Harborough
Milton Keynes
Newport
Newton Abbot
Norwich
Oban
Ormskirk
Petersfield
Portsmouth
Poole
Redhill
St Albans
St Andrews
St Neots
St Helier
Salisbury
Sheffield
Stafford
Staines
Stevenage
Sutton Coldfield
Teddington
Tenterden
Tiverton
Torquay
Trowbridge
Truro
Tunbridge Wells
Twickenham
Walsall
Wilmslow and
Alderley Edge
Wells
Weston-super-Mare
Windsor
Witney
Woking
Worcester
Yeovil

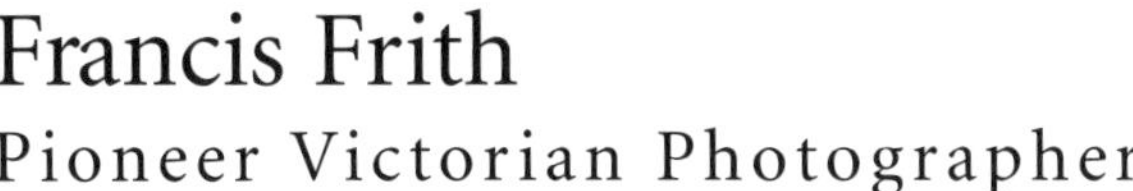

Francis Frith, founder of the world-famous photographic archive, was a complex and multi-talented man. A devout Quaker and a highly successful Victorian businessman, he was philosophical by nature and pioneering in outlook. By 1855 he had already established a wholesale grocery business in Liverpool, and sold it for the astonishing sum of £200,000, which is the equivalent today of over £15,000,000. Now in his thirties, and captivated by the new science of photography, Frith set out on a series of pioneering journeys up the Nile and to the Near East.

He was the first photographer to venture beyond the sixth cataract of the Nile. Africa was still the mysterious 'Dark Continent', and Stanley and Livingstone's historic meeting was a decade into the future. The conditions for picture taking confound belief. He laboured for hours in his wicker dark-room in the sweltering heat of the desert, while the volatile chemicals fizzed dangerously in their trays. Back in London he exhibited his photographs and was 'rapturously cheered' by members of the Royal Society. His reputation as a photographer was made overnight.

By the 1870s the railways had threaded their way across the country, and Bank Holidays and half-day Saturdays had been made obligatory by Act of Parliament. All of a sudden the working man and his family were able to enjoy days out, take holidays, and see a little more of the world.

With typical business acumen, Francis Frith foresaw that these new tourists would enjoy having souvenirs to commemorate their days out. For the next thirty years he travelled the country by train and by pony and trap, producing fine photographs of seaside resorts and beauty spots that were keenly bought by millions of Victorians. These prints were painstakingly pasted into family albums and pored over during the dark nights of winter, rekindling precious memories of summer excursions. Frith's studio was soon supplying retail shops all over the country, and by 1890 F Frith & Co had become the greatest specialist photographic publishing company in the world, with over 2,000 sales outlets, and pioneered the picture postcard.

Francis Frith had died in 1898 at his villa in Cannes, his great project still growing. By 1970 the archive he created contained over a third of a million pictures showing 7,000 British towns and villages.

Frith's legacy to us today is of immense significance and value, for the magnificent archive of evocative photographs he created provides a unique record of change in the cities, towns and villages throughout Britain over a century and more. Frith and his fellow studio photographers revisited locations many times down the years to update their views, compiling for us an enthralling and colourful pageant of British life and character.

We are fortunate that Frith was dedicated to recording the minutiae of everyday life. For it is this sheer wealth of visual data, the painstaking chronicle of changes in dress, transport, street layouts, buildings, housing and landscape that captivates us so much today, offering us a powerful link with the past and with the lives of our ancestors.

Computers have now made it possible for Frith's many thousands of images to be accessed almost instantly. The archive offers every one of us an opportunity to examine the places where we and our families have lived and worked down the years. Its images, depicting our shared past, are now bringing pleasure and enlightenment to millions around the world a century and more after his death. For further information visit: www.francisfrith.co.uk

FREE PRINT OF YOUR CHOICE

Mounted Print
Overall size 14 x 11 inches (355 x 280mm)

Choose any Frith photograph in this book. Simply complete the Voucher opposite and return it with your remittance for £2.25 (to cover postage and handling) and we will print the photograph of your choice in SEPIA (size 11 x 8 inches) and supply it in a cream mount with a burgundy rule line (overall size 14 x 11 inches). **Please note: photographs with a reference number starting with a "Z" are not Frith photographs and cannot be supplied under this offer.**
Offer valid for delivery to one UK address only.

***PLUS:* Order additional Mounted Prints at HALF PRICE - £7.49 each** (normally £14.99) If you would like to order more Frith prints from this book, possibly as gifts for friends and family, you can buy them at half price (with no additional postage and handling costs).

***PLUS:* Have your Mounted Prints framed**
For an extra £14.95 per print you can have your mounted print(s) framed in an elegant polished wood and gilt moulding, overall size 16 x 13 inches (no additional postage and handling required).

IMPORTANT!

These special prices are only available if you use this form to order. You must use the ORIGINAL VOUCHER on this page (no copies permitted). We can only despatch to one UK address. This offer cannot be combined with any other offer.

Send completed Voucher form to:
The Francis Frith Collection, Frith's Barn, Teffont, Salisbury, Wiltshire SP3 5QP

CHOOSE A PHOTOGRAPH FROM THIS BOOK

Please do not photocopy this voucher. Only the original is valid, so please fill it in, cut it out and return it to us with your order.

Picture ref no	Page no	Qty	Mounted @ £7.49	Framed + £14.95	Total Cost £
		1	Free of charge*	£	£
			£7.49	£	£
			£7.49	£	£
			£7.49	£	£
			£7.49	£	£
			£7.49	£	£
			* Post & handling		£2.25
			Total Order Cost		£

Please allow 28 days for delivery.
Offer available to one UK address only

Title of this book ....
I enclose a cheque/postal order for £ ....
made payable to 'The Francis Frith Collection'

OR please debit my Mastercard / Visa / Maestro / Amex card, details below

Card Number

Issue No (Maestro only) Valid from (Maestro)

Expires Signature

Name Mr/Mrs/Ms ....
Address ....
....
....
.... Postcode ....
Daytime Tel No ....
Email ....

ISBN: 1-84567-742-0 Valid to 31/12/08